Judaism

adapted by Amy Zavatto

ALPHA

A member of Penguin Group (USA) Inc.

Adapted from the original series published as *Religions of the World*, published by Penguin Group (USA) Inc., publishing as Prentice Hall, Copyright © 1999 Laurence King Publishing Ltd.

The Pocket Idiot's Guide to Judaism published by Penguin Group (USA) Inc., publishing as Alpha Books, Copyright © 2003, Laurence King Publishing Ltd.

International Standard Book Number: 0-02-864481-6
Library of Congress Catalog Card Number: 2002113268

04 03   8 7 6 5 4 3 2

Interpretation of the printing code: The rightmost number of the first series of numbers is the year of the book's printing; the rightmost number of the second series of numbers is the number of the book's printing. For example, a printing code of 02-1 shows that the first printing occurred in 2002.

Printed in the United States of America

Contents

Introduction

The point of this book is not to be the end-all, be-all study on the Jewish faith (we couldn't possibly fit all that into this tiny little package—maybe not even a hundred of these tiny little packages). But it does give you the basic rundown of the larger groups within the faith, a brief history of the Jewish people, an explanation of holidays and celebrations, and a lot of extra little bits and pieces of info along the way in the form of useful sidebars. Speaking of …

The Word

Here, you'll find definitions of important terms that maybe you've heard before, or they might be completely new to you.

Testament

Important facts about the Jewish faith and history.

Did You Know?

Extra information that will enrich your understanding of Jewish history and culture.

Trademarks

All terms mentioned in this book that are known to be or are suspected of being trademarks or service marks have been appropriately capitalized. Alpha Books and Penguin Group (USA) Inc. cannot attest to the accuracy of this information. Use of a term in this book should not be regarded as affecting the validity of any trademark or service mark.

Chapter 1

Who Is a Jew?

In This Chapter

- What Jewish law says about who's Jewish and who isn't
- To convert or not to convert ...
- Jewish communities all over the world
- The State of Israel

Whether you're a non-Jew trying to learn more about this rich religious and cultural tradition, or you are Jewish and attempting to brush up on the ideas and traditions of the Jewish community, everyone has to start at the beginning—and so do we. The most obvious place to kick-off is with the most obvious question: Who is a Jew?

Mother's Side

According to *halakhah* (Jewish law), a person is Jewish if he or she has a Jewish mother. Anyone who can trace a straight matrilineal descent from a woman who was accepted by the community as a Jewess is considered a Jew.

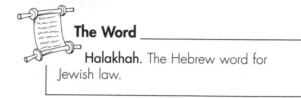

The Word

Halakhah. The Hebrew word for Jewish law.

Although if you're an outsider (or, for that matter, even an insider), this might not seem entirely fair. Even so, this definition has held three notable advantages:

1. It is clear and easy to understand.

2. The identity of a baby's mother is seldom a matter of debate since pregnancies and birth are almost invariably witnessed; paternity, on the other hand, is a far trickier matter.

3. In the long history of abuse and persecution of the Jewish community worldwide, any baby conceived as a result of rape could still be counted within the Jewish fold. Because Jewishness is a matter of physical descent, personal religious belief is irrelevant to status. It is quite possible to be a believing Muslim or Christian and still be a Jew, according to Jewish law.

However, modern life has complicated matters of Jewish law and some groups have changed the traditional definition. Statistically, Jewish men are more likely to "marry out" of the faith than are Jewish women. The National Jewish Population Survey of 1990 showed that the total out-marriage rate was running at approximately 57 percent. A recent decision of the American Reform movement reflects this change. (In the next chapter, we'll discuss the many breakdowns of the faith, including the Reform movement.) The Reform Rabbinical Association declared that the child of one Jewish parent (whether father *or* mother) is under the presumption of Jewish status and that the child of a Jewish father must be regarded as Jewish provided he or she had some form of regular Jewish education. Sounds great, right? Well, it gets a little more complicated than that: The decision is unacceptable to the Orthodox and Conservative Jews who still adhere to the tradition of matrilineal descent.

 Testament

> According to the *Mishnah*, the anthology of Jewish law compiled in the second century C.E., "Thy son of an Israelite woman is called thy son, but thy son by a heathen woman is not called thy son."

Still, the Knesset, the Israeli elected assembly, produced another definition in Israel by passing the Law of Return, which stated unequivocally that "Every Jew has the right to come to this country [Israel] as an immigrant." It went on to define Jew as a person who "was born of a Jewish mother or who had become converted to Judaism and is not a member of another religion." Close family members of such people are entitled to become Israeli citizens under this law as well.

As this law doesn't really define the nature of conversion to Judaism, all those who have come into the fold through the non-Orthodox movements are counted as Jews. By allowing non-Jewish family members, Gentile spouses and children and many who cannot produce evidence of strict matrilineal descent can be included. This brings us to our next question ...

Who Can Become a Jew?

It *is* possible to convert to Judaism (we'll go into more detail on conversion in Chapter 10). As already stated above, in the more traditional groups, a convert (and her children if the convert is a women) will be accepted into the religion but will not be recognized as a Jew. The *Talmud* describes the process:

> The rabbis say: Now if someone comes and wants to be a convert they say to him: Why do you want to be a convert? Don't you know that the Jews are harried, hounded, persecuted, and harassed and that they suffer many troubles? If he replies: I know that and I am not worthy, then they receive him without further argument.

The Word _____

Talmud. A Compendium of Oral Law compiled in Palestine in the late fifth century and in Babylon in the sixth century.

However, non-Jewish spouses do convert to Judaism all the time. Often, a Jewish boy falls in love with a non-Jewish girl. He wants to marry her, but he also wants to have Jewish children. The Orthodox accept converts, but they insist that the conversion must be the result of a desire to be Jewish, not from a desire to be married. The Progressive groups, on the other hand, are more accommodating. They believe that if Judaism is to survive, converts must be welcomed. These synagogues and temples provide regular conversion courses.

Did You Know? _____

For many centuries, the Christian Church deemed it a capital offense for any Christian to convert to Judaism. For their part, Jews have the obligation to follow the whole *Torah* in all its complexity. So, it seemed way-back-when that there was no practical advantage to becoming a Jew, and there seemed to be no point in encouraging converts.

The Word

Torah. The first five books of the Old Testament, which include Genesis, Exodus, Leviticus, Numbers, and Deuteronomy. The Torah is also known as the Pentateuch.

Obviously, the vast majority of those converted to Judaism in this and the last century have come through Progressive organizations. The sticky part about this is that the Orthodox do not recognize these people as Jews. As far as they are concerned, these converts are still Gentiles and, if they are women, their children will also be Gentiles. Today there are many members of Reform and Conservative synagogues who perceive themselves as Jews, who raise their children as Jews, who are regarded as Jews in their own communities, but who are seen as non-Jews by the Orthodox.

Did You Know?

The Torah teaches that even apostates (those who renounce their faith) who have deliberately rejected the faith, remain Jews if their mother is Jewish.

Many Faces, Different Places

Although in 1948 Israel was founded as the official Jewish state, the vast majority of the Jewish community has lived outside of the Promised Land for the last 2,500 years. Before the start of World War II in 1939, it was estimated that world Jewry numbered approximately 16.5 million. Of this, 7.5 million lived in Eastern Europe (Poland, Austria-Hungary, the Balkans, Russia, and the Baltic States), one million in Asia, half a million in Africa, and 5.5 million in the New World.

The largest Jewish community was in Eastern Europe. Here, Jewish religious life flourished. Many Jews lived in *Shtetls*, small towns predominantly inhabited by Jews where the common language was Yiddish. In these towns, young men studied the Talmud in famous *Yeshivot*, traditional rituals were practiced in the home, and day-to-day life revolved around the synagogue and the home. As people emigrated to the larger cities of Eastern Europe like Warsaw in Poland, Vienna in Austria, and Odessa in southern Russia, Jews began to assimilate more into secular society. Many climbed the social rungs of their host society, becoming prominent lawyers, doctors, journalists, and so on. (Unfortunately, not everyone was happy about these inspired, ambitious new members of their communities and feelings of anti-Semitism among non-Jewish fellow citizens began to fester.)

The Word

Shtetl. Small Eastern European towns mainly inhabited by Jews.

Yeshivot. The plural for Yeshiva, an academy where students study the Torah.

By the early twentieth century, Shtetls slowly began to erode as America became the destination of choice. The United States offered new opportunities to these Eastern European Jews. It is estimated that between 1840 and 1925 more than 2.5 million people of Jewish origin entered the United States as immigrants.

It was an ugly and shocking event that was the true destructor of the Jewish traditional way of life in Eastern Europe—the catastrophe of the Nazi Holocaust. The figures tell a grim story: By 1948, world Jewry had been reduced from 16.5 to 11.5 million. Of these, nearly six million lived in the United States. The Jews of Western Europe numbered only approximately one million; there were less than one million in Eastern Europe, nearly two million in the Soviet Union, and about half a million in the new State of Israel.

Since then, the population of Israel has substantially increased, but still a new pattern has been established. The United States remains the home of the largest, richest, and most powerful Jewish community in the world. It is almost twice as large as that of the State of Israel, which comes second in size. Unlike the United States where *Ashkenazi* Jews (Jews of Eastern European origin) are prominent, Israeli society is approximately half and half Ashkenazi and *Sephardi* (Asian Jews). (More on this in Chapter 4.) Third in line is that of the states of the former Soviet Union. Here, however, Jews have been denied knowledge of their religious and cultural heritage during the years of the Communist Regime.

The Word

The Dispersion. From the Greek word *diaspora*, the term given to the Jewish communities living outside of the Land of Israel.

The best example of the fullness and diversity of Jewish life in the *Dispersion* is in the United States. Although not many families have been in the United States for more than three or four generations (and, as in Israel, their forebears come from all over the world), the influence of Jews in the Great American Melting Pot is undeniable. The variety of institutions is astounding. There are synagogues representing every shade of religious and social opinion, including prayer groups for feminists and homosexuals. There is the whole spectrum of generous Jewish charities, liberally performing *mitzvahs* and supporting good causes in their communities and throughout the world at large.

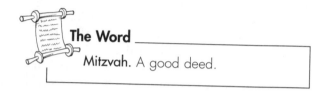

The Word

Mitzvah. A good deed.

In every major American city there are Jewish retirement homes and blocks of sheltered housing for the elderly and handicapped. There is a Jewish Family Agency, Jewish hospitals, and a Jewish burial society. The community supports innumerable educational establishments, varying from strictly Orthodox Yeshivot to Progressive Jewish day schools, from synagogue nurseries to kosher summer camps. For young adults there are Jewish Community Centers offering a wide range of leisure activities, Jewish country clubs, libraries, museums, and extensive programs of adult education.

The fourth largest Jewish community in the world is in France, which has approximately 600,000 Jews. This is a particularly interesting population because it is a meeting of two distinct cultures. Although the old Ashkenazi community was decimated by the occupying Nazis during World War II, the survivors were joined by a large influx of Sephardi Jews from North Africa. Today, more than half of all French Jews live in Paris, which has been described as the largest and most lively center of Jewish life in all Europe.

Did You Know?

One of the most important and moving museums of Jewish history—as well as the most vital reminder of why anti-Semitism is a plague that needs to be wiped from the Earth once and for all—is the Holocaust Museum in Washington, D.C. It is a journey through a horrible time in our history (and one you'll need to block out several hours of your day for; it is not quick trip through a building), but one that everyone should experience.

Great Britain escaped Nazi domination in World War II, and its Jewish institutions survived intact. Today there are slightly less than 300,000 Jews in Britain, the majority of whom belong to the Orthodox United Synagogue under the leadership of the Chief Rabbi. Although most identify themselves as having an Orthodox lifestyle, individual Jews have risen to powerful positions in the government, in commerce and industry, in the general white-collar professions, and in the arts. There is little obvious evidence of anti-Semitism, and the population is well established. In fact, some families are descended from Jews who settled in the country as early as the seventeenth century.

In Asia there are approximately half a million Jews living as far apart as Turkey in the west and China in the east. A synagogue was built in Hong Kong in the 1990s.

The Jews of India are a particularly fascinating group as they claim to have come to the country in biblical times, and there are several old communities that seem to have had no contact with each other until the eighteenth century. In certain places, there is a caste system that distinguishes between white and black Jews, and, until recently, there was no intermarriage between the subgroups.

There are more than 300,000 Jews living in Canada, nearly a quarter of a million in Argentina, and an equal number in the rest of Latin America. The community of South Africa numbers over 100,000 and there are more than 70,000 Jews in Australia. All these populations have their own special characteristics. Some communities are ancient and others were created largely by refugees from Nazism.

North Africa has several ancient and important Jewish communities. In recent years, however, they have been greatly depleted. After Algeria became independent of French rule, the majority of Jews left, either for France or for Israel. Large-scale emigration has taken place from Tunisia and the important, historical community of Cairo (Egypt has been reduced to a few hundred Jews). Even in Morocco, where the king has frequently expressed his wish that his Jewish subjects live in peace and prosperity, the community has shrunk from over 200,000 to approximately 20,000.

However, the African group that has captured newspaper headlines is that of Ethiopia. No one knows the true origin of the Jews of Ethiopia, but they themselves claim to be the descendants of King Solomon and the Queen of Sheba. There was some doubt as to their authenticity, but in 1973 the Israeli Chief Rabbinate pronounced them to be Israelites, and two years later they were declared to be eligible for Israeli citizenship under the Law of Return.

The Jewish community is an international one. Many members have strong feelings of patriotism and identification with their native countries, but at the same time, they share a sense of common history and experience. Jews are of many different races; they come from a wide variety of socioeconomic circumstance; they are conscious of being a single people and the idea of *K'lal Israel* (the whole of Israel) is very important to them, even if they disagree on what that means.

The State of Israel

The establishment of the Jewish state in 1948 was seen by many as the fulfillment of a religious dream. Every year at the spring festival of Passover after the ritual meal has been eaten, the participants promise, "Next Year in Jerusalem!" For the first time in nearly 2,000 years since the end of Jewish sovereignty over Palestine in the first century C.E., this hope can actually be fulfilled.

Nazi anti-Semitism and the Holocaust effectively destroyed the old Jewish communities of Eastern Europe. Those who survived the concentration camps all too often found that there was no place for them in their old homes. Israel became the ultimate goal and destination, and, once the new state had come into existence, about two thirds of those Jews who had been languishing in the Displaced Persons' Camps settled there.

Since then, the Israeli population has increased enormously. In 1946, there were approximately 600,000 Jews living in the land. By 1989, according to official calculations, the Jewish population was more than 3.5 million. In the last decade, this figure has been swollen by immigrants from the former Soviet Union. This increase took place in spite of the three devastating wars of 1956, 1967, and 1973, constant military danger, and almost insurmountable economic problems.

By no means are all Jewish immigrants Holocaust survivors. Israel was, in effect, created by Jewish immigration, by a willingness to use weapons in self-defense, and, ultimately, by a resolution of the United Nations. The surrounding countries— Egypt, Jordan, Syria, and Lebanon—were implacably opposed to having a Jewish state in their midst. In consequence, there was an enormous rise in Arab anti-Semitism. The lives of Jews in many Islamic countries—the Sephardim Jews—became intolerable and emigration to the Promised Land, as Israel is known, became an attractive proposition. There has been large-scale immigration from Turkey, Iraq,

Syria, Lebanon, Iran, Yemen, and the countries of North Africa. In addition, the imagination of the world has been captured by the arrival of black Jews from Ethiopia and by large numbers of Jews from the former Soviet Union, who are also fleeing from a long tradition of anti-Semitism.

Although there are Jews in Israel from many different countries and from the whole spectrum of religious observance, the electoral system of proportional representation has given strictly Orthodox Jews considerable influence there. The system enables them to retain their control over the rabbinical courts and to prevent the introduction of civil marriage and divorce. They receive financial support from the state for their own schools, which concentrate on religious subjects. There are numerous Yeshivot and seminaries, and, through the Ministry for Religious Affairs, synagogues and religious courts are funded by the government. There are two Chief Rabbis, who are state functionaries, one representing the Ashkenazim and the other the Sephardim.

 Testament

The Ministry in Israel is controlled by Orthodox Jews and, despite the presence of progressive seminaries and synagogues, the non-Orthodox movements receive no government money and are fiercely opposed by the religious establishment.

Many Israelis, however, have little time for the traditional Jewish religion. The separation between the secular and the strictly Orthodox schools does little to help mutual understanding. The aggressive stance taken by some of the young Orthodox Jews on such matters as maintaining Sabbath observance (they have been known to throw stones at moving cars) and preventing archaeological digs (Jewish law forbids the exhumation of corpses) is quite understandably condemned by secular Israelis. The strictly Orthodox are exempt from military service on religious grounds. Even Orthodox Jews who *do* serve in the army occasionally have secular conflict where their commitment to the Torah (as they see it) collides with their loyalty to the state. The extreme example was the assassination of Prime Minister Yitzhak Rabin by an extremist Yeshiva student in November 1995, which outraged the public.

However, Israel remains a Jewish state and the focus of the Jewish world. Despite its many problems—social, military, economic, and religious—it inspires enormous loyalty. As the traditional Passover liturgy puts it, "This year we are here: next year we will be in the Land of Israel. This year we are slaves; next year we will be free ..."

The Least You Need to Know

- The strictly Orthodox only accept someone as a Jew if they are born of a Jewish mother or they have converted to Judaism under their auspices. However, the more liberal groups not only allow their own conversion, they are willing to allow those with only a Jewish father to be considered as Jews.

- Because of the horror and devastation of the Holocaust, the focus of the Jewish world has changed from Europe to Israel and the United States.

- The State of Israel, created in 1948, is the Promised Land for many Jews; however, not everyone—even in Israel—sees eye-to-eye on matters of what it means to be truly Jewish.

Chapter 2

Let's Break It Down

In This Chapter

- In the strictest sense: Orthodoxy
- Melding into modern society: Reform
- Finding a balance: Conservative
- Additional branches on the tree

What does it mean to say you are Jewish? Well, as a matter of fact, it can mean a lot of things. Some practicing Jews are extremely conservative and strictly follow Jewish law, while others are more liberal. Let's take a look at the myriad ways Judaism is practiced.

The Strictly Orthodox Tradition

Let's start with strict Orthodoxy, as this particular group within Judaism is the most immediately and physically identifiable one. The strictly Orthodox are a small but immediately recognizable group. The men wear dark suits, black hats, and ritual fringes. The women and girls follow rules of modesty: Skirts cover the knee, sleeves come over the elbow, necklines are high, and stockings are always worn. Their lives are governed by the numerous provisions in the Torah. The Orthodox tend to live close together in self-defining communities, always within walking distance of their synagogue (during the Sabbath, no cars are used).

Following the Rules: The Roles of Men and Women

Almost all the men attend services daily (some even twice daily), and there is strict separation between the men and the women in the synagogue building. Studying the Jewish law in the Torah is largely reserved for men while the women maintain the very traditional role of caring for and keeping the home thriving and stable.

Men and women marry young in their teens or very early twenties, and most get started on child-bearing immediately as a large family is regarded as a blessing. (Except in cases of medical necessity, use of birth control is discouraged.) Even sexual relations are regulated by the Torah. For instance, during her monthly period and for seven days afterward, a woman is not permitted to have sex with her husband. At the end of a woman's menstruation, she bathes herself in the community ritual bath (*mikveh*) and only then can marital relations be resumed.

The Word

Mikveh. A bathhouse where Orthodox women ritually cleanse themselves after menstruation.

Growing Up Strictly Orthodox

The children attend Jewish schools where boys and girls are taught separately and eventually follow a different curriculum. In addition to secular studies, they learn Hebrew and study the Jewish sacred books, but by the time they've reached their teens, education for boys and girls go in different directions.

The boys read the Talmud, the massive compendium of Jewish law compiled in Babylonia in the sixth century C.E. When they graduate from their Jewish high school, young men don't go on to secular universities like other high school students across America. Instead, the boys attend a *Yeshiva* in which Jewish knowledge is the sole subject of study. The girls go on to a seminary that has a modified curriculum and will ultimately give them some sort of teaching certificate.

During these years, under the careful supervision of their elders, the young people will meet to get to know one another by exchanging local and world views, and engaging in general socializing. Their elders will consult each other and arrange the marital unions for these young people. Thus they will become engaged and marry. For the first few years of married life, most young Orthodox couples are supported by parents and relatives. Only once Talmudic studies are finished and life-long habits established will the young man embark on the serious business of earning a living and providing for his family.

This Is the Modern World: Modern Orthodox

Despite its visibility, strict Orthodoxy is really a very tiny movement. Of the 6 million Jews in the United States, only 3 million identify with a synagogue, and of these less than 300,000 are strictly Orthodox. The majority of American Jews who identify as Orthodox belong to what is called the Modern Orthodox movement. Adherents believe that it's possible to be an observant Jew, but also to be fully in tune with modern culture.

In the synagogues, the regular daily prayer services still take place, and men and women sit separately. The majority of men still wear the skull caps (also called yarmulkes) at all times (when awake and not bathing); however, Modern Orthodox congregants wear more conventional dress than the strictly Orthodox. In addition, many Modern Orthodox Jews adhere to the Jewish food laws (the laws of *Kashrut*—more on this later!)

The Word

Kosher. Food that conforms to the strict food laws found in the Torah, Talmud, and Codes of Jewish law. See Chapter 10 for more details on the kosher rules.

Life is different for Modern Orthodox children, as well. They may attend Jewish schools, but they will be institutions where secular subjects are every bit as important as Jewish studies. Even more of a departure from strict Orthodoxy, graduates can and do go on to conventional universities, and a woman is free to pursue a career in her chosen profession. Another important difference is that unlike the strictly Orthodox who may have arranged marriages, the Modern Orthodox young people choose their own marriage partners (generally within the community), and it's unusual for them to marry before their mid-twenties or before their schooling is complete. Modern Orthodox couples also do not tend to have an exceptionally large number of children.

Despite all these concessions to modern Western lifestyles, the Modern Orthodox movement teaches that the Jewish law, the Torah, is the inspired Word of God and that it was originally given to the Prophet Moses when he stood before God on Mount Sinai. As Samson Raphael Hirsch (1808–1888), the founder of the Orthodox movement, declared:

If our religion so commanded us, we would abandon so-called civilization and progress. We would obey without question because we believe that our religion is the true religion. It is the word of God, and before it every other consideration must yield. The Jew has to judge everything by the unchangeable touchstone of his God given law. Anything that does not pass this test does not exist for him.

Branching Out: Other Groups Within Judaism

Although the Orthodox control the religious establishment in the State of Israel, and they are a powerful force in the United States and Europe, many Jews have rejected what they see as a sort of fundamentalist view of Judaism. Instead, they set up alternate institutions and modes of worship, which in their opinion better express the essence of Judaism. These movements are as follows:

- Reform
- Conservative
- Reconstructionist
- Humanistic
- Modern Zionist
- Progressive

What follows is a brief look at each of these fascinating and important movements in the Jewish faith.

Remake, Reform

In the nineteenth century, biblical criticism and the increased opportunities available to Jews in the secular world brought about two important movements: the Reform and Conservative movements.

The Reform movement began in the early nineteenth century and encouraged religious diversity, free thinking, and personal autonomy. Members of the Reform movement concentrated on stressing the ethical dimension of Judaism. In Orthodoxy, they argued, Judaism had become too inward-looking. But now, in an age when Europe was becoming more and more liberal, it was time for universal Jewish values to be shared more openly with Christians and even nonreligious fellow countrymen. If that meant diluting the form of actual worship, as the Orthodox accused them of doing, then that's the way it would have to be.

Reform Jews emphasized the importance of sharing their views—or, as they called it, the Prophetic tradition. They saw themselves as making Judaism more relevant to the modern Jew, who now had at least one foot in general civic society. They saw the ethical guidelines of the Ten Commandments as a more important aspect of Judaism and they rejected what they viewed as the outdated laws concerning animal sacrifice, ritually pure food, and other customs that distinguished Jews from their non-Jewish fellows.

As with any movement in history, though, it wasn't long before the Reform movement itself began sub-dividing into groups that favored moderate change and those that embraced radical change. For the latter, abandoning Hebrew in favor of the local vernacular in synagogue services, eliminating prayers that overemphasized the particularity of the Jewish people, and even in some cases moving the Sabbath from Saturday to Sunday were some of the more extreme overhauls of traditional Orthodoxy proposed.

What's in a Name? The Conservative Movement

Another group that rejected strict Orthodoxy was Conservative Judaism, the American movement that followed later in the nineteenth century. This group accepted that some changes were inevitable, but it tried to reach a compromise between Reform and Orthodox. In the United States today, the majority of those who belong to a synagogue—about three million—choose to join either a Conservative or a Reform congregation.

The Conservative Jews have important differences in belief and practice from those in the Reform movement. As their name implies, the Conservative Jews are more reluctant to depart from the age-old traditions than are those who embrace the Reform movement.

Testament

In other countries, like Great Britain, France, and Hungary, similar controversies developed, which created different groups. For example, in Great Britain, the more traditional organization called itself Reform, while the more radical is called Liberal.

Despite their differences in acceptance of modern life, both Reform and Conservative Jews accept the findings of modern biblical scholarship. In other words, adherents don't believe (as the Orthodox do) that the Torah was literally dictated by God to Moses. Instead they see it as a collection of traditions originating at different times in ancient Israel that was divinely inspired, but, at the same time, was the product of developing human reflection.

This means that non-Orthodox Jews deem themselves entitled to adapt, or even to reject, certain provisions of Jewish law if they conflict with modern life. So, when the rabbis of the American Reform movement established their principles at a conference in Pittsburgh in 1885, they declared, "We accept as binding only the moral laws and maintain only such ceremonies as to elevate and sanctify our lives, but we reject all such as are not adapted to the views and habits of modern civilization."

Since then, the Reform movement has grown, developed, and even flourished. Today, Reform Jews prefer to allow their members to obey or disobey the food laws as a matter of personal choice. They believe in the absolute equality of men and women and have rejected the laws of purity and divorce as being disadvantageous to women. Girls and boys receive exactly the same religious education and, in recent years, both the Conservative and the Reform movements have ordained women as rabbis.

More Branches on the Tree

But that's not all, folks. Just as there is an abundance of small and large groups under the umbrella known as Christianity, so there are in Judaism as well. The twentieth century saw two other movements come into being. Reconstructionism grew out of Conservative Judaism. Its founder, Mordecai Kaplan (1881–1983), taught that Judaism should be understood as an evolving civilization that includes both religious and secular elements. Kaplan proclaimed that belief in God was no longer necessary, and synagogues should reconstruct themselves as centers for all aspects of Jewish culture.

But hold onto your hat—things get more radical still with Humanistic Judaism. This movement originated in Detroit, Michigan, in 1969 under the leadership of Rabbi Sherwin Wine (1928–). He teaches that Judaism, like all other religions, is a purely human creation that is always changing; it embraces many beliefs and lifestyles, and Wine extols the humanistic dimensions of the faith. The Society of Humanistic Judaism believes that:

- Each Jew has the right to create a meaningful Jewish lifestyle free from supernatural authority (yes, that means God) and imposed tradition.
- The goal of life is personal dignity and self-esteem.
- The secular roots of Jewish life are as important as the religious ones.
- The survival of the Jewish people requires a reconciliation among science, personal autonomy, and Jewish loyalty.

Embracing Ethnicity

Even with all this debate raging among the groups within Judaism, there is yet another factor to consider: Many Jews have no religious affiliation whatsoever. About 50 percent do not belong to a synagogue, do not send their children to religious school, marry outside the faith, and freely enjoy all the advantages of a secular, twenty-first century lifestyle.

Even without religious parameters, many of these people still identify themselves as Jews and believe they are completely Jewish. Some extol this by getting involved in Jewish communal causes—like joining the campaign to help Soviet Jewry, giving to charities, or supporting educational institutions.

Other affiliate with their Jewishness by learning the Yiddish language of their Eastern European fore-fathers or by listening to East European Jewish klezmer music. Yet others feel that by participating in general causes of social justice—such as the Civil Rights movement or a commitment to the Jewish State of Israel—they are living out the ethical obligations of their Jewish heritage. Among secular Jewry, it is commonplace to hear the justification, "We're not religious, but we do support Israel."

Did You Know?

The Modern Zionist movement, begun by Austrian journalist Theodor Herzl (1869–1904), draws on the ancient Jewish belief in the return to the land of Israel. Herzl believed that anti-Semitism was endemic in European Christian society and that Jews would never be safe as a minority group in a foreign land. Furthermore, to achieve freedom, Jews must have a land of their own.

Today the whole Jewish community, Orthodox, Progressive, and secular, are united in their determination that the political State of Israel, which was created to provide a homeland for the Jews after the war, must survive. But even with all the differences in worship and tradition, each of these sects is yet another fiber in the beautiful tapestry that makes up Judaism.

The Least You Need to Know

- Orthodox Judaism is the strictest group within Judaism in which the Torah is followed to the letter and communities remain close.

- In response to the confines of Orthodoxy in the modern world, Reform Judaism seeks to meld in with secular society while keeping true to their Jewish heritage.

- Conservative Jews try to strike a balance between the Orthodox tradition and the looser-ruled Reform movement.

- Many other groups of Judaism have emerged over the years—some, like the Humanists, believe that God is not a necessary component of being Jewish.

Chapter 3

That's Ancient History!

In This Chapter

- Who were the Israelites?
- The bravery of the three Patriarchs—Abraham, Isaac, and Jacob
- Moses' role in the survival of the Jewish people
- The struggle to find—and hold onto—the Promised Land
- Learning to live with trouble—the Romans

It has been said that we can't predict the future if we don't look at our past. The Jewish faith is an age-old one that has seen much struggle and change throughout time. In this chapter, we'll go back to the beginning (or as far back as we know!) to give you a historical look at where it all began (and later, we'll talk about where it's going).

Judaism in Biblical Times

The Israelites are the ancestors of the Jewish people, and their history is largely based upon the stories recounted in the *Tanakh*), the Hebrew Bible. The first five books of the Bible are known as the Pentateuch (the Torah), and it is in the first book, Genesis, that the essentials of the Jewish faith—God's creation of the world—are explained.

Did You Know?

Christians have their own name for the Tanakh; they call it the Old Testament and incorporate it into their own scriptures.

Scholars aren't entirely certain of the historical accuracy of these Biblical accounts of events, people, and genealogies in the Torah. Why, you ask? Well, as in our modern world, science and religion tend to have different versions of the past, and the stories of the Torah can't be supported by archaeological findings or by references to the Israelites in the writings of peoples in neighboring lands. But of course, this is where the basis of most religions comes into play: faith.

> **The Word**
> **Patriarchs.** Those believed to be fore-
> fathers of the Jewish people. They are
> Abraham, Isaac, and Jacob.

Honest Abe

The Jews believe they are descendants of the *patriarch* Abraham, who is guesstimated to have lived
sometime between 1700–1900 B.C.E. Abraham was
a native of the Middle Eastern city of Ur in present-
day Iraq. So the story goes: God promised that if
Abraham left his comfortable life, he would become
the father of a great nation. Even though he and
his wife were getting on in years and they were
childless, Abraham accepted the call and became
a nomadic herdsman.

Encouraged by his elderly, apparently barren wife,
Abraham had a son, Ishmael (c. 1850 B.C.E.), with a
slave woman. Ishmael was to become the father of
the Arab people. Against all expectation, Abraham's
elderly wife, Sarah, produced her own son, Isaac
(c. 1850 B.C.E.), who did indeed become a patriarch
like his father.

The Word

Covenant. A special agreement that the Jews believe is made between God and the Jewish people.

A *covenant* relationship was established between God and Abraham. God promised that he would protect and preserve Abraham's family, that they would be as numerous as the stars of heaven, and they would be His Chosen People. On their part, Abraham's descendants must obey God's commandments (not such a bad deal!).

Testament

In the Jewish faith, the practice of circumcision was instituted as a symbol of the covenant: "Every male among you shall be circumcised .... It will be a sign of the covenant between you and me .... He that is eight days old among you shall be circumcised." To this day, the practice remains a basic article of faith.

Isaac went on to have a son of his own, Jacob (c. 1750 B.C.E.), who became the third patriarch. Jacob was also given the name of Israel ("One who has striven with God"). Later, Jacob took his entire family and settled in Egypt. He was the father of

12 sons who, in their turn, were the fathers of the Twelve Tribes of the Jewish people. Initially they had been privileged immigrants, but, as described in the Book of Exodus, "There arose a new king over Egypt who did not know Joseph [Jacob's second youngest son]." The Egyptians enslaved the Israelites and set them to building cities.

Let My People Go: Moses

The thing about injustice is that, eventually, something's got to give. And in the case of the Israelites, change manifested itself in the form of a young man named Moses. Although he was Jewish, Moses supposedly was brought up in the pharaoh's court. Despite his semi-fortunate circumstances, he could not bear the injustices being done to his people, and he was inspired by God to lead his people to freedom.

According to the Hebrew Bible, God sent a series of 10 plagues on Egypt. The last one was the death of all the first born children of the land. To avoid this calamity, the Israelites were instructed by God to kill a lamb and smear its blood on the doorposts of their homes. On seeing the stain, the Angel of Death would "pass over" the house. The Egyptians were so frightened and horrified by this last plague, that they finally released the Jews from bondage and allowed them to leave.

The Israelites then gathered their possessions together, not even allowing time for their bread to rise, and fled the country. This event is still celebrated by Jews today as Passover (or *Pesach*).

Did You Know? _____

Passover is one of the most important festivals of the Jewish faith because it is a celebration of freedom. For eight days, to commemorate the haste with which their ancestors fled ancient Egypt without allowing time for their bread to rise, Jews eat nothing made with a raising agent. You may have seen one of the more popular unleavened items in your grocery store around the time of this festival, matzoh bread. The festival begins with a dinner at which the story of their ancestors' escape from slavery in Egypt is told again.

For 40 years, the fugitives wandered in the desert of the Sinai Peninsula. It was during this time that Moses received the ultimate revelation from God. On Mount Sinai, he was given the Torah, the book that contains the Jewish law and, in turn, the basis of the Jewish faith. This is enshrined in the Pentateuch, the first five books of the Jewish scriptures, which include the following books:

- Genesis
- Exodus
- Leviticus
- Numbers
- Deuteronomy

Did You Know? _____

The Orthodox believe that the Torah was literally dictated by God to Moses. Reform and Conservative Jews adopt what they see as a more flexible position, in that they don't necessarily believe that Moses and God had a sit-down about the Torah. For all Jews, though, the Torah is the foundation of their religious life.

King Me

Thank goodness for tenacity—it took them 40 years, but eventually, the Israelites' conquest came to an end in Canaan (what is now modern day Israel), which was seen as God's Promised Land. Despite various forms of leadership in the tribes throughout the years, the need for a king became apparent. The first king chosen by the Twelve Tribes was a young man named Saul (eleventh century B.C.E.), but he committed suicide after a devastating battle and subsequent defeat inflicted by a neighboring nation. He was succeeded by David (tenth century B.C.E.), who conquered the city of Jerusalem and made it his capital. It is said that God promised He would establish David's descendants to hold the throne forever through all generations.

Testament

Jews still believe that God will send a new king—the Messiah (the anointed one)—to bring about divine rule on Earth, and the chosen one will be descended from David.

David's son, King Solomon (c. 930 B.C.E.) built the magnificent Temple in Jerusalem, which was dedicated to God. Here daily sacrifices were offered in praise of the Almighty and in atonement for Israel's sins. However, after the death of Solomon, the Twelve Tribes split up. The ten northern Tribes split away from the two southern Tribes and established their own kingdom. During the period of the Divided Kingdoms (930–722 B.C.E.) many of the Biblical prophets were at work. Elijah (ninth century B.C.E.), Hosea, Amos, Micah, and Isaiah (all eighth century B.C.E.) warned the people of impending disaster. They were convinced that God would punish His people because they ignored His word, led wicked lives, and were not faithful to the covenant.

Did You Know?

So the story goes: It is said that the prophet Elijah was so powerful and important that he did not die, but was taken up to Heaven in a fiery chariot. It is still believed by the Orthodox that he is waiting to return to herald the days of the Messiah.

Doomed to Be True

The prophecies proved to be all too accurate. In 721 B.C.E., the Assyrians (from modern day Iraq) destroyed the Northern Kingdom and the 10 northern Tribes disappeared from history. Although legend maintained that they still survived in some faraway region and could yet be gathered together in the days of the Messiah, the reality is that they intermarried with neighboring tribes and lost their national and religious identity. And that wasn't the end of it. In 598 B.C.E. the Babylonians, the successors of the Assyrians, conquered the two southern Tribes (Judah and Benjamin). Heartbreakingly enough, they went on to destroy King Solomon's Temple in Jerusalem, and they took the Jews into exile.

And thus, the Promised Land was snatched away. But all was not completely lost from this devastating experience. Sustained partly by the words of the Biblical prophets and by the Law of the Torah, the Jews survived. The prophet Ezekial comforted the people who remained alive by reminding them of God's faithfulness: "I will rescue them from all places where they have been scattered on a day of cloud and thick darkness. And I will bring them out from the peoples, and gather them from the countries and will bring them into their own land."

Back to Basics

During the 70 years of exile from the Promised Land, the Jewish leaders tried to rebuild hope for the future. They looked for a kingly figure, a messiah, who would restore the nation to its former glory and put an end to all human conflict. More important, this period marked the flourishing of the prophets, who were none too happy with what they saw as a dismantling of Jewish traditions. The prophets condemned Jews for adopting pagan practices and chided the people of Israel for their past misdeeds. They insisted that they return to the true spirit of the Law, and not just go through the motions of empty rituals that, they felt, were becoming devoid of ethical obligations. They also warned of the dangers to Jewish identity in a political arena full of enemies.

From this, Jewish leaders seemed to have developed the practice of meeting together on a regular basis. They could no longer offer sacrifices because the Temple that was destroyed by the Babylonians was the only proper place for that, but they could come together to pray and study the Torah.

Did You Know?

This type of gathering, which began out of necessity, started a very important tradition that carries on to this day. It is an important feature in Jewish religious life as we know it—it was the start of the synagogue as an institution.

Less than 70 years later, the Babylonians were conquered by the Persians (from modern-day Iran).
Although many chose to make a life in the com-
forts of Babylon, a group of the faithful struggled
back to the Promised Land. Under the leadership
of Zerubbabel (a descendant of David) and the priest
Haggai, they rebuilt the Temple. It was on a far
smaller scale than the previous building, but sacrifice could be resumed. However, from that time
on, there were two centers of world Jewry: Judaea
(the old Southern Kingdom) centered on Jerusalem,
and the Dispersion with its center in Babylonia.

Things were not easy for the returned exiles, but
the situation was transformed by Nehemiah (fifth
century B.C.E.) who was appointed governor of the
land in 445 B.C.E. The scribe Ezra (fifth century
B.C.E.) gathered the people together and read the
Law to them. The listeners were transfixed by the
words of the Torah and were immediately determined to keep the festivals prescribed in it:

- *Pesach* (Passover)
- *Shavuot* (weeks)
- *Sukkot* (tabernacles)

These were agricultural celebrations as well as
commemorations of God's goodness in liberating
the Jews from slavery, giving Moses the Law, and
preserving the Israelites in the wilderness. Ezra,
however, took his back-to-basics approach to a
more severe length and insisted that Jewish men
who were married to "foreign" wives divorce them so

that the land would be purged of outside influences. Even today, the strict Jews see their faithfulness to the Torah and their aversion to intermarriage as the cornerstones of ethnic and religious survival as a people.

The Second Temple and the Dispersion

The Babylonians had not taken the entire Jewish population into Babylon, only the leaders, the affluent, and influential people. The "people of the land" had been left behind. They intermarried with people of other settled populations, but they retained their belief in one God. When the exiles returned, these people known as Samaritans had been eager to stress their relationship with the Jews and had offered to help rebuild the Temple, but the Jews did not want their assistance. Once the Samaritans saw that they were not accepted as Israelites, they developed their own, separate traditions. A small group survives to this day. They insist that their version of the Torah is the correct one and that their High Priest is descended from the family of Moses' brother Aaron, the first High Priest.

The Word

Samaritan. Descendants of the inhabitants of the Northern and Southern Kingdom who intermarried with the surrounding peoples during the Babylonian exile.

In 333 B.C.E., the Samaritans were given permission
to build their own temple on Mount Gerizim. They
claimed that this was the only place where it was
permissible to offer sacrifice and that it was chosen
by God. This temple was destroyed by Jewish forces
around 128 B.C.E., but the Samaritans continue to
offer the Passover sacrifice on their mountain and
to practice their ancient form of Israelite religion.

Judaea itself continued to be occupied by foreign
powers. In 333 B.C.E., the King of Persia was
defeated by Alexander the Great (352–323 B.C.E.)
of Macedonia (Northern Greece). Alexander's aim
was to spread Greek culture throughout the world.
He conquered a huge empire that extended from
Greece to the borders of India and included Egypt
and Babylonia. When he died of fever, his lands
were divided between his many generals. However,
greed got the best of these men, and they fought
over the lands for 20 years, reducing their number
to only three generals of the original group:

1. Ptolemy I founded the Ptolemaic dynasty in
   Egypt.
2. Seleucus I founded the Seleucid dynasty in
   Mesopotamia.
3. Antigonus I founded the Antigonid dynasty
   in Asia Minor and Macedonia.

Initially, Judaea was under the control of the
Ptolemies of Egypt. The Ptolemies were basically
tolerant of Jewish religious practice, to the point
that there was a thriving Jewish community in the
city of Alexandria on the Nile delta. Although these

Egyptian Jews remained faithful to the God of their ancestors, they spoke Greek and enjoyed a fairly assimilated lifestyle. Alexandria was also the home of the eminent Jewish philosopher, Philo (c. 25 B.C.E.–40 C.E.), who tried to integrate Greek philosophy and Jewish religious teaching into a unified whole.

 Testament

> The Hebrew scriptures were first rendered into Greek in Alexandria; the translation was known as *Septuagint.*

By 198 B.C.E. a Seleucid king, Antiochus III (reigned from 223–187 B.C.E.), had taken over Judaea. He, however, did not share the tolerant attitude of his predecessors and was determined to turn Jerusalem into a Greek city. Various measures were introduced such as Greek Games in which the athletes competed naked (a totally abhorrent practice to those following the Jewish tradition). The next monarch, Antiochus IV (reigned from 175–163 B.C.E.) was even more insensitive. He occupied the city, banned circumcision, and plundered the Temple treasures. He rededicated the building to Zeus, the king of the Greek gods, and he ordered that the sacrifices should include pigs, which the Jews regard as ritually unclean (or unkosher).

Inevitably, all this led to conflict between those Jews who wished to liberalize Jewish practice—the Hellenizers—in the interest of greater assimilation with the Greek world, and the Jewish traditionalists led by the priest Mattathias (d. c. 167 B.C.E.) and then by his sons (most notably, Judas, also known as Maccabee the hammer, d. c. 160 B.C.E.). Even though Antiochus' army supported the Hellenizers, the traditionalists succeeded in recapturing Jerusalem. Their first priority was to cleanse the Temple and to rededicate it to God.

 Testament

> Supposedly, when the traditionalists went to cleanse and rededicate the Temple, there was only enough holy oil to sustain the great light inside it for one day, but miraculously it lasted for eight. Today the Jewish community lights candles for eight days to celebrate this victory of the Jews over foreign influences, and they call this celebration *Hanukkah*.

Mattathias's descendants succeeded in founding a dynasty of both rulers and High Priests, and the Seleucid kings were compelled to acknowledge the independence of Judaea. The kingdom was extended to include Idumea, Galilee, and northern Trans-Jordan, and the inhabitants of all these areas were compelled to convert to Judaism. But despite this great success, the Jewish empire took yet another hit.

When (Not) in Rome ...

By the middle of the first century B.C.E., the Romans had annexed Judaea and had turned it into a client state. Herod (73–4 B.C.E.), the son of an Idumean military governor of Judaea under the Romans, was an official in Galilee. When the Romans were expelled by the Parthians, Herod fled but returned with a Roman army in 37 B.C.E. to reconquer Judaea. He was then made King of Judaea by the Romans and ruled until his death. Despite being a Jew by religion, he was detested by his people as a usurper.

Nonetheless, he did a great deal for the country. He built the port of Caesarea (named for his Roman master, Caesar); he negotiated various privileges for the Jews of the Roman Empire; and he rebuilt the Temple on a splendid scale. This new incarnation of the Temple was magnificent—it contained an outer court where everyone, Jew and non-Jew could mingle, another court for Jewish women, a further court for male Israelites, and a court of priests where the hierarchy was able to again offer the daily sacrifices. The innermost sanctuary was the Holy of Holies. This was hidden from sight by a curtain, and it was only entered once a year by the High Priest on the Day of Atonement (*Yom Kippur*). There he would beg God's forgiveness on his people.

The Temple was tended to by the hereditary priests. They were said to have been descended from Moses' brother, Aaron. They upheld the complete authority of the Pentateuch, and they rejected the permanent validity of a body of oral interpretations of the law. As a result, they did not believe in such doctrines as the resurrection of the dead since these developed as a result of discussing the complicated implications of the Biblical text.

Did You Know?

Today the Yom Kippur, with its preceding Ten Days of Penitence, remains the most solemn season of the Jewish year.

Testament

The priests were drawn from a group known as the Sadducees, who were possibly named for Zadok (tenth century B.C.E.), the High Priest of King Solomon who had also served under King David. They are mentioned in the New Testament and are described by the historian Josephus (c. 38–c. 100 C.E.).

The priests were not a very large group, but, as the aristocrats of the Jewish nation, they had a great deal of influence on the people, and as the group most in authority had to deal with the Romans. The Pharisees were quite different. They were described as scribes and sages, and they were famous for their verbal interpretations of the sacred books. Regularly in the synagogues, they expounded the deeper meanings of the scriptures and, as the self-appointed moral leaders of the people, they devised a complex body of oral law over the years. By the first century B.C.E., every Judaean village contained a synagogue where the people could gather together and listen to the Pharisees' sermons.

But change was on the horizon once again. A growing hostility between the rich and the poor, a series of famines, and an increased sense of messianic fervor all added to a boiling pot of change. Most notably, one new religious sect that began to grow and gain popularity among the people followed a man named Jesus of Nazareth whom they believed to be the son of God. They claimed that the Kingdom of Heaven was dawning and, after Jesus was crucified, they hailed their martyred leader as the promised Messiah, believed in his resurrection, and in time broke away from other Jews to become a distinct and separate religion—Christianity. These events were recorded in what became the Christian New Testament, or the Gospels, and today Christianity is the world's largest religion.

More Setbacks

Matters came to a head in 66 C.E. The Zealots, a sect of freedom fighters and political guerillas, raised a revolt and took control of the city of Jerusalem. This didn't sit well with the Romans, who subsequently sent armies in from the north and laid siege to the city. By late summer 70 C.E., the daily sacrifices were yet again suspended, and on August 24 the beautiful Temple of Herod went up in flames. After the devastation, all that remained standing was the extreme Western Wall.

Did You Know?

The Western Wall remains the most sacred place in the Jewish world and is a destination of pilgrimage. Even secular Jews return to the land of the forefathers to say their prayers (some write the name of a person whom they are praying for and secure the paper in one of the cracks in the wall) or just to stand in awe in front of this piece of Jewish history.

Meanwhile, the Zealots continued to hold out in the south at the fortress of Masada. When the rebellion was finally subdued, the Romans held a triumphal procession through the streets of Rome displaying the spoils of the Temple. This is recorded on the Arch of Titus, which still stands in the Roman forum (marketplace).

Despite this new setback, the Jews were not discouraged. A rebellion against Rome was waged in 132 C.E., but it was put down by 135 C.E. Around this time the Roman emperor Hadrian converted Jerusalem into a pagan city and forbade Jews from living there. He also renamed the province of Judaea as Palestina (you guessed it—Palestine) after the Jews' old enemy, the Philistines—a deliberate attempt to obliterate the connection between the land and the Jewish people.

Scholars regard this setback as the last blow and definitive end of Jewish political sovereignty in the Promised Land—at least for the next 1,800 years or so. The Jews had to come to terms with the new religious system, which could no longer be centered on the Temple, the priesthood, and sacrifice. By this stage there were Jewish colonies in all the major urban centers around the Mediterranean Sea. Increasingly, the Jewish religious establishment was to concentrate on the needs and developments of these growing Dispersion communities.

The Least You Need to Know

- The Israelites are the ancestors of the Jewish people and their story is recounted in the Hebrew Bible, the *Tanakh*.

- The three Patriarchs—Abraham, Isaac, and Jacob—are believed to be the forefathers of the Jewish people.

- Moses, a Jew raised in the court of the pharaoh, was disgusted with the enslavement of his people and led them out of Egypt to find the Promised Land, modern-day Israel.

- Despite their struggles to maintain the land, various unsympathetic forces—most notably, the Romans—eventually wrestled the sacred land from the possession of the Jews.

Chapter 4

Growth and Challenge

In This Chapter

- The beginning of Rabbinic Judaism
- How Christianity planted the most fertile seeds of anti-Semitism
- Survival in Europe and the Middle East
- The story of the Sephardic and Ashkenazi Jews

Change is inevitable in our world—and 2,000 years ago, change was nearly as expected as a breeze from the sea. So, it's not so surprising that several important sects of Judaism and Christianity began to grow and challenge each other's ways of life and points of view. In this chapter, we'll look at the growth of Rabbinic Judaism, Christianity, and the resulting peoples from these sects.

Leaders of the Pack: Rabbinic Judaism

After the Temple was yet again destroyed, it wouldn't have been so shocking for Judaism to disappear like so many of the cults in the ancient world. Its survival was largely due to the vision and dedication of the *Pharisees*.

The Word

Pharisees. A religious sect of the Second Temple era who were scrupulous in obeying the written and oral laws of the Jewish faith.

During the siege of Jerusalem, Rabbi Johanan ben Zakkai (first century C.E.) escaped from the city and founded an academy on the coast at Javneh. There groups of scholars gathered to discuss, develop, and preserve the legal tradition. Under Johanan's successor, Gamaliel II (early second century C.E.), the supreme legal body of the Jews, the Sanhedrin, was re-established and the learned came from far and near to listen to and participate in the debates. The canon of scripture was decided, regular daily prayers were organized, and a system of rabbinical ordination for Jewish leaders was established.

In the rebellion of 132–135 C.E., these organized religious activities were temporarily halted and the Javneh academy was transferred to Galilee. By the second century C.E., the oral interpretations of the law had become highly complex and Judah ha-Nasi (the patriarch) set himself to the task of recording the debates and decisions on each particular topic. His official position and authority allowed his book of legal opinions, the Mishnah, to become the officially accepted one. The text of this great law book is divided into six orders:

- *Zeraim*—dealing with the laws of agriculture
- *Moed*—dealing with the laws of Sabbaths, fasts, and festivals
- *Nashim*—dealing with the laws of marriage and divorce
- *Nezikin*—dealing with civil and criminal law
- *Kodashin*—dealing with the laws of temple ritual and sacrifice
- *Tohorot*—dealing with the law of ritual purity

However, Judah ha-Nasi's recordings were not merely a summary of the conversations around him. He recorded the debates with the minority view expressed first ("Rabbi Simeon says …"), and each account ends with the final conclusions ("But the sages declare …"). It is an astonishing piece of work and by accomplishing it, Judah ha-Nasi provided a solid foundation upon which further discussions could be based.

At that time the Jewish leaders were also preoccupied with the proper interpretation of the scriptures. The rabbinic interpretation of Holy Writ is known as *Midrash*. Since the Pentateuch is regarded as the Word of God, it became vital that it should be correctly understood, especially since so much disruption had plagued the Jewish people. By studying and debating, the rabbis could define Jewish law precisely. For example, they decided that there were 39 different types of work to be avoided. These include harvesting and kindling a fire, which is why Orthodox Jews today will neither pick a flower nor turn on an electric light during the Sabbath.

Meanwhile, other scholars founded centers elsewhere. In Galilee there were well-known academies in Tiberius, Caesarea, and Sepphoris. The Jewish community of Babylonia was not to be left behind, however. There the king recognized the Jewish community leader and gave him the title of Exilarch. This was a hereditary office, and its holders claimed to be related to King Jehoiachin (sixth century B.C.E.), the last Judaean king of Davidic descent.

At the same time, famous Babylonian schools of learning were established at Sura in Central Mesopotamia and Pumbedita on the river Euphrates to study the Torah. The heads of these academies were called Gaons. Together with the Exilarch, the *Gaonim* controlled the powerful Babylonian community. There scholars were not known as rabbis; this was a title only bestowed by the laying on of hands at ordination and it only applied in Judaea. Babylonian authorities were known as Rab (Rav).

By the end of the fourth century C.E., the rabbis of Judaea had assembled the teachings of further generations of scholars on four of the six orders of the

Mishnah. The additional material was described as *Gemara* (completion) and the whole is known as the Palestinian (or Jerusalem) Talmud. The same work was being accomplished in Babylonia. The Babylonian Talmud was completed in the sixth century C.E. It is nearly four times as long as its Palestinian counterpart and is considered to be more authoritative. Not only does this text record the legal judgments and debates, it contains information on medicine, history, science, and agriculture. There are proverbs and fairy tales, folk legends, and rules of etiquette. Throughout the Middle Ages, it was the main study of the Babylonian academies and it spread throughout the Jewish world.

Did You Know?

The title of rabbi is used somewhat differently today. Now, a rabbi is one learned in Jewish law, who has been ordained to teach and preach, and who generally serves a congregation full-time. The Judaean and Babylonian scholars almost invariably had secular occupations from which they gained their livelihood. Only in the Middle Ages did the title "rabbi" come to mean the spiritual leader of a particular Jewish community.

The Word

Exilarchate. The heads of the Babylonian Jewish community from the first to the thirteenth century C.E.

Did You Know?

To this day, Talmud remains the main text in the Orthodox Yeshivot schools. Even though many of its provisions are no longer relevant—such as those pertaining to the temple and priesthood—they are still read. Within the Orthodox community today, Talmudic study remains a lifetime commitment.

Put It in Writing

Not all Jews at the time were excited about the development of the oral law. In the days of the Temple, the aristocratic Sadducees believed that only the written law was authoritative and that later oral interpretation could be ignored. Despite the efforts of the Palestinian and Babylonian sages, this strand of opinion survived within the community. In c. 760 C.E., Anan ben David, who had been passed over for the Exilarchate, set up his own alternative movement. Anan's principle was, "Search thoroughly in the Torah and do not rely on my opinion." He insisted that the whole law was to be found in the scriptures and not in rabbinical interpretation. Gradually the movement spread. Adherents were known as the Karaites and, by the tenth century, communities were established in Egypt, North Africa, Persia, Babylonia, and Palestine. However, the rabbis remained devoted to oral law and resisted Anan ben David's teachings. By the sixteenth century, the Karaites' numbers were in decline.

Did You Know?

When the State of Israel was established in 1948, the Karaites were regarded as eligible for immigration under the Law of Return. Today there is a community of approximately 7,000 Karaites living in Israel who maintain their own customs, have their own ritual butchers, and support their own religious court. However, by both the laws of Israel and their own custom, they are not allowed to intermarry with the Israeli population.

The Growth and Challenge of Christianity

We know that by the first century C.E. there were Jewish communities in all the major cities of the Mediterranean. However, there was another sect growing in popularity at the time—one that would even further challenge the Jewish faith's ability to hold on: Christianity.

By the fourth century C.E., Christianity had become the official religion of the Roman Empire. Christians felt that their New Testament added to and completed the Old Testament that was held so dear by the Jews. As Christian theology developed, it emphasized that by accepting the Kingship of Jesus, Christians—and no longer the Jews—were the elected nation of God. From this, an irreparable rift developed between them and their Jewish antecedents.

The early Christians believed that they were the true inheritors of the privileges of Israel and that the Jews were hard-hearted and blind in their rejection of what they considered the true Messiah (of course, to the Jews, the Messiah had not—and still has not—arrived). But things got much worse than that. By the time the Christian Gospels were written, the Jews were perceived as demonic. To drive this point further, the New Testament writers seem to have interpolated conflicts between Jesus and the Jewish leaders into their narratives, and—in the most damning blow—blamed the Jews for the death of Jesus ("His blood be on us and on our children"). Thus, the seeds were sown for nearly 20 centuries of Christian anti-Semitism.

Conflict on the Continent

In Christian Europe, Jewish communities were self-contained units, and Christian rulers allowed each area to establish its own rules. By the tenth century, there were important centers of Jewish learning in Northern France and in the Rhinelands. Jews had also settled in England at the time of the Norman Conquest in 1066, and there were small communities throughout France and the Holy Roman Empire (present day Netherlands, Germany, and Austria). Yet Jewish existence in Christian Europe was never secure. The Church continued to teach that it was the Jewish people alone who were responsible for the death of Jesus Christ, and there were periodic outbreaks of violence against the Jewish European communities.

The situation was made worse by the Crusades. By the eleventh century, the Muslim Turks were in control of the Holy Land (Jerusalem) and the Christian holy places. The princes of Europe were encouraged by the Church to send armies to fight the Infidel, or the Muslims. If it was meritorious to slaughter Muslims abroad, then it seemed only logical to harass the Jews at home. Both groups were considered infidels because they did not accept Jesus as the Messiah. And just when you thought things couldn't get any worse, the Black Death raged through the continent in the fourteenth century, and the Jews were widely (and ludicrously) accused of causing the disease by poisoning the wells.

But things got worse—much worse. As early as 1144, the Jewish community of Norwich, England, was charged with using the blood of Christian children in the manufacture of Passover unleavened bread. The Blood Libel, as it was called, spread throughout Europe. The entire community was expelled from England in 1290; a few years later the French king evicted all the Jews from the French crown lands. In 1298, Christian mobs destroyed approximately 150 Jewish settlements in Germany. Then, in 1492, after the Christian monarchs Ferdinand and Isabella had driven out the Muslim rulers from Spain, they also exiled the ancient and successful Jewish community from their dominions.

This made the hospitality of Poland seem very attractive. From the thirteenth century on, the Jews have been protected there. They were used by the great Polish nobles to collect taxes and manage the huge estates. The religious wars of the Protestant Reformation and the Catholic Counter-Reformation in the sixteenth century also led to the migration to Poland of Jews from central to Eastern Europe. By the end of the sixteenth century, the Jewish communities of Poland and the Baltic States were the largest and most powerful in Europe, where they were allowed communal autonomy.

In the Iberian peninsula, there were Jewish poets such as Judah Halevi (1075–1141), Moses ibn Ezra (c. 1055–c. 1135), and Solomon ibn Gabirol (c. 1021–1056), and philosophers such as Bahya ben Joseph ibn Pakuda (c. 1050–1120), Abraham ben David Halevi ibn Daud (c. 1110–1180), and

Hasdai Crescas (1340–1412). Most famous of all
was Maimonides (Moses ben Maimon, 1135–1204).
He not only produced a comprehensive codifica-
tion of the corpus of the Jewish law (the Mishneh
Torah), but his philosophical work, *The Guide to the
Perplexed*, set the tone for all subsequent debate.
However, the glory of Spanish Jewry was not to
last. After Spain was conquered by the Christians,
there was a period of uncertainty. Then, in 1492, all
the Jews were expelled from Spanish soil. The only
way to remain in their homes was to receive the
Christian sacrament of baptism. The members of
this rich, cultured and successful Jewish community
were scattered. Some went to North Africa, some
to Italy, some to Holland, and others to Turkey.

The Word

Yiddish. A German and Hebrew
language written in Hebrew characters
that became the common language of
the Eastern European Jews.

Meanwhile, Back in the Middle East ...

In other Muslim countries, Jews had fared differently. The founder of Islam in southern Arabia,
Muhammad (c. 590–632), was widely accepted
among the Muslims as God's prophet. He had hoped
that the Jews would accept his message. Like them,

he taught that God is One, and he adopted certain Jewish rituals such as a fast day, similar to the Day of Atonement (Yom Kippur). Like the Jews, the Muslims do not eat pork, maintain fixed times for prayer, and reject the worship of images. Much of Muhammad's original legislation was similar to Jewish *halakhah* (law) and, like the Jews, the Muslims have an extensive tradition of oral law. Nonetheless, the Jews of Arabia were not prepared to acknowledge that Muhammad was indeed God's Prophet, and Muhammad became hostile toward them. In particular, the Jewish community of Medina was expelled and destroyed.

Despite this unfortunate beginning, Muslim rulers were tolerant toward the Jews. Since they were monotheists (believers in one God), they were not regarded as infidels, and there was no obligation to fight a holy war against them. Although there were negative incidents, generally the Jews were allowed to live in Muslim territory and enjoy religious freedom. In return for this tolerance, however, they were expected to wear distinctive clothing that marked them as Jews. They were not allowed to make converts, and they were forced to pay an additional annual poll tax.

The Sephardim and Ashkenazim

By this time it was clear that two different Jewish traditions existed side by side. Jews who traced their descent from ancestors who had settled in Christian Europe in the Middle Ages were known as the *Ashkenazim* ("German"). They lived in the German states and, after the persecutions, in Austria, Poland, the Baltic States, and Russia. Meanwhile, those who were descended from the Jews of Spain, North Africa, and Babylonia were known as the *Sephardim* ("Asian").

The Word

Sephardim. Jews descended from those who had lived in Muslim lands.

Ashkenazim. Jews who settled in Northern France, Germany, and Eastern Europe.

Each group fully recognized the other's Jewishness, but they used different liturgical rites and had many different customs. There were local differences even within the broader Ashkenazi and Sephardi communities. The Ashkenazim composed hymns, known as *Piyyutim*, and penitential prayers (*Selihot*). They were known for their piety, their strict adherence to Jewish law, and their Talmudic scholarship.

The Sephardim, on the other hand, were thought to be more open to secular culture and were known for their legal codes and their liturgical creativity. This may have been because their host culture was more open to participation of the Sephardim in their culture. The difference is well illustrated by the seventeenth-century communities of the Dutch city of Amsterdam. The original community was Ashkenazi, but, after the great expulsion, many Spanish Jews settled there. Contemporary engravings of the Spanish and German synagogues show the Spanish congregation as far more affluent, genteel, and worldly (the worshipers almost look as if they are dressed for a gala theatrical performance!). The German synagogue was darker and smaller; the women were banished to a remote balcony and there was an atmosphere of intense piety.

The differences in custom were openly acknowledged. When the Sephardic legal authority Joseph Caro (1488–1575) published his great code of Jewish law, the Shulhan Arukh ("Prepared Table"), Moses Isserles (1525–1572) had to add a supplement to make it acceptable to the Ashkenazim. Despite this, it is remarkable how consistent the essential Jewish laws were in the two communities.

Did You Know?

The population of the modern State of Israel is a mixture of Sephardim and Ashkenazim. When the State was founded in 1948, it was seen primarily as a refuge for the survivors of the Nazi Holocaust—the Ashkenazim. However, many of the Sephardim communities living in Arab-ruled countries were made to feel unwelcome by their rulers and took the opportunity to immigrate.

The Least You Need to Know

- The strict adherence to the Talmud by Rabbinical Jews was a way of maintaining the Jewish culture and religion in an unstable (and often unwelcoming) world.

- Because Jews would not accept Jesus as the Messiah, the seeds were planted for years upon years of anti-Semitism.

- Just as the Jews of Egypt became nomadic wanderers in ancient times, Jews in Europe and the Middle East had to constantly uproot themselves in search of a stable and welcoming home.

Chapter 5

Progress and Regress? Jewish Life Leading up to Modern Times

In This Chapter

- Looking for a new messiah in hard times
- The formation of the Hasidic and Reform movements
- The growth of anti-Semitism
- A new attempt to establish the Holy Land

By the start of the modern period, Jews were established throughout Europe, North Africa, and certain Asian countries. Despite the lessening of anti-Jewish feeling in many places, the large communities of Eastern Europe were to suffer many changes in the seventeenth and eighteenth centuries. Let's take a look at this period in the history of Jewish tradition.

The Arrival of the Messiah?

The security of established Jewish communities in Eastern Europe was interrupted in 1648. In that year, Bogdan Chmielnicki (1593–1657) was elected the leader of the Cossacks, and he led a revolution against the Polish aristocracy. The Jews, some of whom were stewards of the great estates, were considered part of the problem by the Cossacks because of their affiliation with the upper classes. They were massacred in the revolution—probably as much as a quarter of the Jewish population of Poland was murdered during the course of the upheaval and many others were sold in the slave markets of Constantinople (today's Istanbul). Clearly, Poland was no longer a safe place for Jews.

Of course, for every action there is always a reaction. In this case, yearnings for the Messiah to appear grew and grew in the Jewish community from the tragedy they experienced at the hands of the Cossacks in the Chmielnicki revolution. And then came a man named Shabbetai Zevi (1626–1676), a gifted but unbalanced scholar who had attracted many followers. He was born in Smyrna on the Ninth Day of the Av (Av 9), the traditional birth date of the Messiah. By 1665, he had been recognized as the Messiah by Nathan Benjamin Levi of Gaza (1644–1680). Nathan of Gaza (in southern Palestine) believed that he himself was the prophet Elijah.

Levi sent messages throughout the Jewish world, promising that soon the Turkish Sultan would be deposed and that the Twelve Tribes of Israel would be united once more. World Jewry was in an uproar. The date of redemption was set for June 18, 1666. However, when Shabbetai landed near the Ottoman capital of Constantinople, he was promptly arrested. He was taken to the court of the Grand Vizier where he was given the choice between being put to death or converting to Islam. Shabbetai and his wife chose to be Muslims, and he died in exile in Albania.

You'd think this would be the end of the matter, but hold on. Nathan of Gaza continued to insist that Shabbetai was the Messiah and that his conversion was not a betrayal, but instead part of the ongoing battle with the forces of evil. Nonetheless, for most Jews, the whole episode was devastating. Shabbetai was not the Messiah. God had not sent his anointed one to save Israel and the world. It seemed as if Talmudic scholarship and traditional rabbinic learning had failed them. The Jews of Eastern Europe were looking for a new type of Judaism.

Did You Know?

In some quarters, Jews continued to hold Shabbetean beliefs, and some Jews followed their master into Islam, forming the *Dönmeh* ("Apostate sect"). In fact, a Dönmeh community existed in Istanbul until the mid-twentieth century.

Finding the Silver Lining: Hasidim

Eastern European Jews found what they were thirsting for in the teaching of Israel ben Eliezer (c. 1700–1760), known as the *Baal Shem Tov* ("master of the Good Name") or Besht. He grew up in the Carpathian Mountains in present-day Romania, and his mystical preaching attracted a group of followers. He opined that the study of Torah should be an act of devotion and that the whole of daily life could be an offering to God. In particular, he emphasized that worship should be a source of joy; he used to say that his disciples should serve God with gladness since a joyful man is overflowing with love for his fellows and for all God's creatures. The Besht's followers were known as the *Hasidim* ("pious ones"), and the movement spread throughout Eastern Europe. Various new leaders emerged and, in the course of time, leadership became hereditary, handed down from father to son. By the beginning of the nineteenth century, almost half of Eastern Europe's Jewry identified itself with the new movement.

The Word

Hasidim. Adherents to the eighteenth century mystical movement among Eastern European Jews that stresses joy should be part of worshipping God. Important characteristics of Hasidism include rejoicing and enthusiasm.

Hasidim loved to explore the Kabbalah, the main Jewish mystic tradition. Once an esoteric tradition with origins going back to the last days of the Tanakh, it had developed mainly in Sephardi lands. Hasidim tried to open up this previously secret world of ordinary Jews to the Ashkenazim, but most of all, they derived from the Kabbalah the values and attributes of devotion, adherence, wisdom, knowledge, and understanding.

 Testament

> Examples of Kabbalistic books are Sefer Bahir and the Zohar.

It was not long before distinct Hasidic groups arose, each one led by a *Tzaddik* ("Righteous Man"), who is believed to be the spiritual channel through which God's grace flows. By observing the Tzaddik, the Hasid can learn how God can be worshipped in every detail of life, from tying one's shoes, eating one's food, or taking a nap. As the spiritual leader of his community, the Tzaddik speaks to mass audiences, gives individual advice, and is supported by the donations of the faithful. Tales circulated describing the miraculous saintliness of the Tzaddikim and collections of their homilies were published.

Despite the devastation of the Nazi Holocaust, which decimated Eastern European Hasidic populations, the movement survived, particularly in the United

States and in Israel. Adherents are perhaps the most visible segment of the strictly Orthodox community, and the men in particular are readily identifiable by their dress (black hats, beards, side curls, black suits, ritual fringes, and magnificent fur hats on the Sabbath). Among the best-known groups are the *Lubavich*, *Satmar*, *Belz*, *Bobover*, *Gur*, and *Vishnitz* (each named after their town of origin).

Opponents to Hasidim

Not all Jews were persuaded by Hasidism. Many scholars disapproved of the Hasidic deviations from the traditional liturgy, and they were appalled by the Hasidic neglect of painstaking study of the Torah. These traditionalists were known as the *Mitnagdim* ("Opponents"), and their leader was the learned Gaon of Vilna in Lithuania, Elijah ben Solomon Zalman (1720–1797). The Vilna Gaon, as he was called, was himself a child prodigy and was regarded as a master of Talmud at the age of 13. He was determined to preserve traditional scholarship, and he was a major figure in the revival of Talmudic study. There was bitter conflict between the Mitnagdim and the Hasidim. Books were burnt, and decrees of excommunication were pronounced. It went so far that parents would go through the rites of mourning if one of their sons joined a Hasidic sect.

There's a great story about a Mitnag teacher that shows perfectly the difference between the two groups: He was giving a tutorial and two boys were looking out the window at a bird soaring through the sky. When asked what they were thinking, one boy replied that the birds made him think of the soul ascending toward Heaven. To the Mitnag scholar, the reply smacked of Hasidic mysticism and the poor lad was told to leave the class. The other said that he was wondering what would happen if the bird dropped dead and fell on a fence boundary—to whom would the carcass belong? Of course, today the kid would have been sent to the school psychologist as a potential loose canon, but at that time his answer delighted the teacher: "God be praised for someone who knows what religion is about!" he said.

Today, hostility between the Hasidim and the Mitnagdim has largely disappeared. The Hasidim have also become learned Talmudists and, perhaps more importantly, a far greater threat to both these groups emerged with the advent of the Western Enlightenment. The Jews of Western Europe were being freed from their ancient civil disabilities and were being increasingly affected by secular culture. They were beginning to question such fundamental principles as the divine origin of the Torah, which was an abomination to both the Mitnagdim and Hasidim.

Enlightenment and Reform

While the Mitnagdim and the Hasidim were fighting it out in Eastern Europe, great social changes were occurring in the West. In the Holy Roman Empire under Emperor Joseph II (1741–1790), a vital edict of toleration was issued. Jews were no longer to be confined to special places of residence, restricted to their own schools, or made to wear distinctive clothing. Along those same lines, the National Assembly of France granted full citizenship rights of the Jewish population in 1791, and it was agreed that there should be full freedom of religion. Believe it or not, the power-hungry Napoleon (1760–1821) went one step further once he had taken over the French government. In 1806, he convened an Assembly of Jewish Notables and, the following year, he revived the Sanhedrin, the traditional supreme body of Jewish government. From then on, the French Jewish community was organized much as if it were a department of the civil service.

Napoleon himself was defeated at the Battle of Waterloo in 1815, but despite some lingering Christian anti-Semitism, his reforms could not be undone. Several German and French intellectuals argued for the rights of the Jews, and gradually additional freedoms were procured. In 1869, the North German parliament proclaimed Jewish emancipation, and by 1871, all restrictions on occupation, franchise, marriage, or residence were removed. Meanwhile, in England, the Jews had been free to conduct their own religious life as they saw fit since the seventeenth century. Still, various civil disabilities existed that prevented Jews from taking full part in the political and cultural life of the nation. These were all abolished during the course of the nineteenth century, and in 1858, the first Jewish member of Parliament took his seat in the House of Commons.

While these momentous social changes were taking place, the Jews themselves were experiencing an intellectual revolution. The most influential thinker of the Jewish Enlightenment was Moses Mendelssohn (1729–1786). Encouraged by the Christian philosopher G. E. Lessing (1729–1781), Mendelssohn taught that God's existence, His providence, and His gift of immortality could all be discovered by the use of natural reason. He believed that the mission of the Jews was to call attention to the "Oneness" of God and to be a constant reminder to the rest of humanity of the call of ethical monotheism.

Mendelssohn called for freedom of worship and the removal of state interference in religious affairs (as he put it, "Allow everyone who does not disturb the peace … to pray to God in his own way"). He also encouraged the modernization of Jewish education, translated the Pentateuch into German, and wrote an extensive biblical commentary. Through his leadership, German Jewry became acquainted with secular European culture. He himself remained a strictly observant Jew, yet his advocacy of Jewish emancipation brought another dilemma in its wake: How far could a Jew absorb the outside world's culture before he assimilated altogether?

Did You Know?

It's interesting to note that four of Mendelssohn's own six children eventually converted to Christianity.

Give Me Freedom! The Start of Reform Judaism

The Jewish Enlightenment completely changed the lives of Western Jewry. No longer were they restricted in residence (ghetto) or occupation. They became familiar, if not involved, with the ways of the secular world and many came to feel that the traditional ways of worship were no longer suitable. One result of this new free-thinking was the *Reform movement*. Started in Germany, the financier Israel Jacobson (1768–1828) built the first Reform temple at Seesen. There, the liturgy included prayers in German, as well as choral singing. Another similar congregation was started in Hamburg in 1818, which even issued its own prayer book that went so far as to omit all references to the Messiah and to the restoration of the Twelve Tribes to the Holy Land. Members of the Temple saw themselves as loyal Germans and they owed no allegiance to any other place—they had found their home, and a new one was not necessary.

The Word

Reform movement. A progressive denomination of Judaism that has attempted to reconcile the Jewish faith with modern life.

Meanwhile, the departure from traditional Jewry became even more apparent when some religious leaders were denying the fundamental doctrine that the Torah was handed down in its entirety by God to Moses on Mount Sinai. They tried to study the history of Judaism with no religious preconceptions. Others were arguing that Judaism was simply a religious tradition of ethical monotheism and that many traditional practices were no longer valid in modern society. They recommended modifications of the dietary laws, praying with the head uncovered, and even transferring the Sabbath from Saturday to Sunday to be more like their fellow Christian citizens.

Despite the radical thoughts being expressed, many Jews were ready to embrace what they saw as an enlightened, more up-to-date take on their religion. The new movement spread rapidly: The first conference for Reform rabbis took place by 1838; the West London synagogue for Reform Jews was founded in 1841; and a Reform Rabbinical Seminary was opened in Breslau in 1854, another in Hungary in 1867, and the Berlin Hochshule opened its doors in 1872.

The United States eventually became the main center for Reform activities. The first American Reform temple was founded in Charleston, South Carolina, in 1824. Its liturgy was similar to that of the Hamburg temple, and its founders were well-educated Jews. Not long after, Reform temples were built in most major American cities. A new American Reform prayer book was published, and the first conference of American rabbis took place in Phila-delphia in 1869. The Hebrew Union College, the first American Rabbinical Seminary, opened in 1875 in Cincinnati, Ohio.

The principles of American Reform Judaism were laid down in Pittsburgh in 1885. It was agreed that the Jewish tradition would acknowledge the find-ings of modern scholarship, that only the *moral* laws of the Pentateuch were binding for all time, that Jews should no longer look for the coming of the Messiah or the restoration of the land of Israel, and that the dietary laws and the laws of ritual purity were obsolete. By the end of the nineteenth century, many Jews of North America were almost indistinguishable from their fellow non-Jewish citi-zens in dress, manners, education, and aspiration.

A New Twist: Modern Orthodoxy

The Orthodox did not allow this transformation to take place without a fight. They were horrified by the new developments and feared that partici-pating in secular culture could all too easily lead to assimilation—not a desirable side effect to them. However, some compromise seemed to be on the horizon. The best known German Orthodox thinker of the time was Samson Raphael Hirsch (1808–1888), who himself had been educated at the University of Bonn in Germany. Nevertheless, he defended Orthodoxy, arguing that the purpose of life was not to attain happiness, but to serve God. The Torah, he insisted, was indeed given to Moses by God and must be the guiding principle of Jewish life. However, he also believed that it was possible to be fully observant while being in-the-know on modern culture. This position came to be known as *Modern Orthodoxy*. There could be no compromise on the doctrine of the God-given nature of the Torah and the Reform movement must be unequivocally condemned. At the same time, Jews could also have the benefit of a secular education and could enjoy the fruits of modern culture.

The Word

Modern Orthodoxy. Adherents to the more strict denomination of Orthodox Judaism who believe that the Torah was indeed divinely given to Moses and needs to be followed to the letter, but that a certain familiarity with modern culture is acceptable and perfectly safe to engage in.

Although Modern Orthodoxy was highly influential in Western Europe, the Jews of Poland, Russia, and the Baltic States were less affected by it. Western Europe had longer traditions of democratic compromise; by contrast, in the more radical traditions of Eastern Europe, unaffected Jews chose socialist secularism as their preferred tool of protest against Orthodoxy. Change was inevitable, but it was to come not as a result of political emancipation, but in response to anti-Semitism and the opportunity of an entirely new life across the Atlantic.

Anti-Semitism and Zionism

Such a flourishing of Jewish life was occurring all over Europe and the United States that it seemed hopeful that *anti-Semitism* may well disappear into the history books as an ugly lesson to be learned about hatred. It was a great, tragic misfortune that this was not to be the case. Instead, the nature of Jew-hatred altered. In the previous centuries, the Jews were regarded as social outcasts. The Christian Gospels taught that the Jews had rejected Jesus as the Messiah and had sent him to his crucifixion. The vast majority of Christians could not understand why the Jews persisted in their ancient faith since it had been superseded by Jesus' teaching. The Jews were seen as stubborn, obtuse, and blind to God's grace.

The Word

Anti-Semitism. Hatred of Jews.

The very term "anti-Semitism" was not used until the 1870s, and it described a new prejudice. The inventor of the term, Wilhelm Marr (1818–1904), insisted that the Jews were not alien because of their religion, but because they were of a different and foreign race. His twisted views purported that modern history should be understood as an ongoing battle between "native Teutonic stock" and the Semitic foreigner. By 1881, it was being claimed that the Jewish physical type was a threat to the purebred German nation. Jews were described as innately mercenary, egoistic, materialistic, cowardly, and degenerate. These views were spread in such publications as *The Protocols of the Elders of Zion*. This was circulated in Russia from the late 1880s and was supposedly the documents of a Jewish organization bent on world domination.

Did You Know?

Although known to be a forgery, the *Protocols* are still circulated in Russia today and, even more dangerous, have found a new audience in the Arab world and among some fanatic American groups.

In the late nineteenth century, anti-Semitism became an important factor in European politics. In Russia, attacks on the Jews were described as *pogroms*. A pogrom was an onslaught on one sector of society by another, and all too often it included rape and murder as well as the destruction of property. There was a series of pogroms against the Jewish community of Russia between 1881 and 1884 after the assassination of Czar Alexander II (1818–1881).

The Word

Pogrom. An attack, often against the Jews, in nineteenth- and early twentieth-century Russia and Poland.

The civil powers did little to help the Jews—rather, they encouraged this new festering hatred, and many Jews felt that the only safety was in emigration to the New World. A second wave of Russian pogroms occurred between 1903 and 1906, and there was a third outbreak during the Russian Revolution and the subsequent civil war. Altogether, it is estimated that between 1917 and 1921 as many as 150,000 Jewish people were killed by units of both the Red and White Armies. It was not surprising that the Jews of Eastern Europe were anxious to leave. Between 1881 and the outbreak of World War I in 1914, approximately 2 million Jews settled in the United States, a further 350,000 in Western Europe, 200,000 in the United Kingdom, 40,000 in South Africa, 115,000 in Argentina, and 100,000 in Canada.

Western Europe was also not immune to Jew-hatred. In France, the Dreyfus case brought it to international notice. Alfred Dreyfus (1859–1935) was a high-ranking French Jewish army officer who was accused of high treason and sentenced to life imprisonment. He consistently protested that he was innocent, and it was eventually discovered that he was falsely accused; all the evidence stacked against him was based on false documents. Nevertheless, when he was tried again in 1899, a second guilty verdict was returned, and he was only finally vindicated in 1906. Why? Many ludicrously found it impossible to believe that a Jew could also be a loyal Frenchman.

The Search Is Back On: Finding a Jewish State

A young journalist, Theodor Herzl (1860–1904) became convinced after the Dreyfus case that the only solution to anti-Semitism was the foundation of a Jewish State. Palestine was chosen as the potential site for it because this is where Jewry last ruled itself, and because of its Biblical connections. The old dream of returning to the Promised Land was reborn.

Despite the Reform movement, it was still believed by the Orthodox that in the days of the Messiah, the Twelve Tribes would be gathered together again and the Temple would be rebuilt in Jerusalem. As early as 1882, after the first Russian pogroms, a group of Jews had left for Palestine to establish themselves there as shopkeepers, artisans, and farmers. Herzl himself argued for the creation of a Jewish State by international agreement. He convened the First Zionist Conference in Basle in 1897 and devoted the rest of his short life to drumming up diplomatic support. In fact, he was so devoted to the idea that he was willing to consider other locations besides Palestine. The British were prepared to offer a tract of Uganda in Africa to the Jews and, after a visit to the poverty-stricken Jewish villages of Russia, Herzl was so desperate that he was prepared to accept. However, the proposal aroused a storm of protest at the Sixth Zionist Conference and, just before his death, Herzl was forced to affirm his commitment to Palestine.

The small Jewish population in Palestine mainly consisted of religious pilgrims in the Holy Cities and was vastly outnumbered by Palestine's predominantly Muslin Arab population. Also, the land was under Ottoman Turkish rule. Some Zionists, like the British Jewish author Israel Zangwill, seeing the indigenous Arabs as mainly itinerant nomads, called Palestine, "A land without people for people without a land." Others, though, were more far-sighted. In 1891, Ahad Ha-Am warned that Jews would not realize their dreams unless they respected the rights and aspirations of Palestinian Arabs. As he predicted, a clash was inevitable.

There is an old saying that where there are four Jews there are six opinions. This was certainly true in the Zionist movement. The World Zionist Organization, founded by Herzl, was the umbrella body. Socialist Jews also became members of the Poale Zion (the Labor Zionist party). Those of the Orthodox who were willing to participate joined the Mizrakha party, which was dedicated to the preservation of strictly Orthodox ways within the new Jewish State. However, the majority of Western and Eastern (except for the Orthodox) delegates to the Zionist conferences were entirely secular in outlook, and this caused quite a bit of conflict with the Orthodox Jewish establishment in Europe. Prominent early Zionists included Aaron David Gordon (1856–1927) and Chaim Nachman Bialik (1873–1934) who were intent on producing a Hebrew rather than a Yiddish culture, and the socialists Nahman Syrkin (1868–1924) and Ber Borochow (1881–1917) who were encouraging the creation of collective agricultural settlements (*Kibbutzim*) and the growth of trade unionism.

The Word

Kibbutzim. An Israeli agricultural collective. Today, it is not uncommon for young Jewish men and women to go on Kibbutz to Israel to temporarily experience this way of life.

In the early days of Zionism, many of the strictly Orthodox were uneasy about the movement to establish a foothold in Palestine. In 1912, they organized the Agudat Israel to unite rabbis and lay people against the new movement. They maintained that the Ingathering of Exiles (as they referred to it) could not take place until the Messiah had appeared and that it was forbidden to anticipate or to force divine deliverance. Even after the Holocaust, there were those who argued that the Zionist commitment to the ingathering of the displaced Jews of Europe was misguided since it is not possible to determine God's plan for this Chosen People prior to the coming of the Messiah.

After World War I, the newly formed League of Nations agreed that Britain should administer Palestine for the displaced Jews of Europe. In the meantime, the Jewish population continued to grow. In 1917, in the Balfour Declaration, the British government had promised its support for a Jewish State in Palestine. Meanwhile, the Arab inhabitants of the land had become increasingly nervous of Jewish immigration, and by the 1930s, they were launching offensives against the settlers. The situation became impossible. In 1937, a British Royal Commission suggested that Palestine be partitioned between the two groups, but this was rejected in 1939, and Jewish immigration was substantially cut back. Nothing further could be done while the battles of World War II waged. And the greatest calamity of all befell the Jews of Europe ...

The Least You Need to Know

- As a result of atrocities against the successful Jews of Eastern Europe, the beleaguered and weary survivors looked for a messiah—and thought they found him in a man named Shabbetai Zevi.

- Hasidic Jews believe that an important aspect of the Jewish religion is finding joy and enthusiasm in worshipping God.

- The Reform movement began as Jews were assimilated into Western culture. Reform Jews believed that it was possible to be a "good Jew" and yet be thoroughly ensconced in modern culture.

- In the nineteenth century, anti-Semitism again began to grow and paved the way for the future horrors of World War II.

Chapter 6

The Challenge of the Twentieth Century and Beyond

In This Chapter

- How Adolf Hitler's attempt at genocide nearly wiped out all European Jews
- The establishment of Israel and its rocky beginnings
- The struggle between Israel and Palestine
- September 11 and the State of Israel

The blight on world history that is the Nazi Holocaust is a mind-boggling, ugly, corrupt example of how humans can act in very inhuman ways toward one another. It is almost too difficult to conceive of how many lives were lost and, more so, how it could ever have happened in the first place—but happen it did. Blind hatred is a frightening, powerful force that, unfortunately, never seems to be completely obliterated from world history, as we see over and over in examples around the globe.

As we—Jews and non-Jews alike—entered the twenty-first century with hopeful feelings toward the future and peace in the Middle East, the world community was rocked by the horrific terrorist attacks of September 11 and the subsequent unrest that followed between Israel and Palestine. Where will it lead? What does it mean for the future? In this chapter, we will look back at the past and turn a tentative eye toward the future of the Jewish State of Israel.

Hatred Personified: Adolf Hitler and the Nazi Holocaust

In America, we tend to think of the Great Depression as an economic low point in our particular history. Europe was also paralyzed by this period of economic depression, and Germany was hit especially hard. Between 1930 and 1933, more than six million people were unemployed there and the government was unstable. It was this chain of down-trodden events and several ineffective coalitions that led to the appointment of Adolf Hitler (1885–1945) as Chancellor in 1933.

Hitler was the leader of the National Socialist Party, the Nazis; his ideology was based on a fusion of anti-Communism and anti-Semitism. He was convinced that all Jews were degenerates and parasites, and he argued in his book, *Mein Kampf* ("My Struggle"), that it was the treachery of the Jews that caused Germany to lose World War I. He perceived the Jews as a demonic people who were seeking world-wide domination. As he himself put it:

The black-haired Jewish youth lies in wait for hours on end, satanically glaring at and spying on the unsuspicious girl whom he plans to seduce, adulterating her blood and removing her from the bosom of her own people ... the Jews were responsible for bringing Negroes into the Rhineland, with the ultimate intention of bastardizing the white race which they hate and thus lowering its cultural and political level so that the Jew might dominate ....

Once the Nazis gained power, a series of anti-Jewish regulations came into force. Among them ...

- Jews were deprived of citizenship.
- Jews were forbidden to marry or have sexual relations with German citizens.
- All Jews were compelled to register their property.

The Violence Begins

On the night of November 9, 1938, anti-Jewish sentiment took a fateful—and plotted—turn. The Nazi government organized a concerted attack on all Jewish businesses and communal institutions. Synagogues were burnt to the ground, shops were destroyed, and many individual Jews were murdered. The events of the *Kristallnacht* (the Night of Broken Glass) made it clear to the Jews of Germany that they could expect no mercy from the Nazis.

The Word _____

Kristallnacht. Translated from German means, "The night of the broken glass." This fateful event, in which Jewish businesses and synagogues were attacked and burnt to the ground and many Jews were murdered, began a long and horrible period of anti-Semitism.

Realizing that this was likely not going to be an isolated event, many Jews tried to find a means of escaping from the country with their families, but it was not easy. The United States, also in the throes of the Great Depression, had many unemployed citizens and was accepting very few new immigrants. The British had curtailed Jewish settlement in Palestine, and the countries of Western Europe were not inclined to take in any more refugees. All too many, however, were forced to stay, and once World War II broke out in September 1939, there was no escape.

Testament _____

Families resorted to desperate measures, sending their children abroad without them to distant relations or sending them on *Kindertransports* (child-transports) to save their lives.

The German armies overran Europe, and everywhere they continued their merciless persecution of the Jews. In Poland, there still remained a large Jewish population despite some previous migration, and Jews there were seized and forced to participate in a massive work program that was little more than imprisonment and slave labor. They were forced to toil seven days a week, were dressed in little more than rags, and to say they were given totally inadequate rations is to be generous with words.

Once the Nazis had invaded Russia in 1941, special squadrons known as the *Einsatzgruppen* were co-opted to deal with the Jews. In each conquered town, the Jews were rounded up, marched out to the countryside, and shot.

 Testament

It has been estimated that between October 1941 and December 1942, 1.2 million people were murdered by the Einsatzgruppen squadrons.

From Bad to Worse

The despicable murders by the Einsatzgruppen squadrons were only the tip of the iceberg—even these murders were not sufficiently systematic or efficient for the Nazi leaders.

At the Wannsee Conference on January 20, 1942, the "final solution of the Jewish question" was outlined and explained, and history took an even darker turn. A network of concentration and extermination camps was set up. Jews from all over Europe were rounded up and deported for "resettlement" in the east.

Initially, they were crammed into ghetto areas in the major cities, but from there they were transferred to the concentration camps. In the camps of Chelmno, Auschwitz, Sobibor, Majdanek, Treblinka, and Belzec, the young and fit were selected for work where they lived in miserable conditions in a state of perpetual fear, cold, and hunger. Once they became too weak to labor, they, too, experienced the same fate as the elderly, the infirm, and the children who were sent to the gas chambers to be mercilessly murdered.

 Testament

> The camp at Auschwitz in southern Poland could hold 140,000 prisoners and had five crematoriums that could dispose of 10,000 bodies a day.

The whole operation was conducted with ruthless efficiency and even when Germany was clearly losing the war, nothing was allowed to hinder the transportation of Jewish civilians to the camps. Altogether, it has been estimated that six million Jews died in this Holocaust.

In many places, the Jews did their best to resist. There were several small-scale rebellions in the concentration camps, and the inmates of the Warsaw ghetto held out for several weeks against the might of the German *Reich*. Nonetheless, in most places the Jews were poor, isolated, and surrounded by hostile neighbors. It seemed that they had been abandoned by the rest of the world. Despite Germany and the Nazi regime's inevitable demise, by the end of World War II European Jewry had effectively been decimated, and the old synagogues, Yeshivot, and centers of Jewish learning were destroyed forever.

End Game

The demise of Eastern European Jewry brought about a renewed and stronger demand for a rewarded land for Jews. World Jewry rallied to the Zionist cause. Jews had fought in the British, United States, and Canadian armies during World War II but the question of what to do for the refugee concentration camp survivors remained unsolved. Meanwhile, the situation in Palestine that had begun in the earlier twentieth century (see Chapter 5) came to a boil. A sizeable sector of the Jewish population, under the leadership of Menahem Begin (1913–1992), were prepared to employ terrorist tactics against the British administrators in order to procure what they felt was rightfully theirs.

On November 6, 1944, Lord Moyne, the British minister for Middle Eastern Affairs, was assassinated. A rift developed between the leader of the World Zionist Organization, Chaim Weizman, and Begin over the bombing of the King David Hotel in Jerusalem, but the campaign of violence continued and culminated in the hanging of two British army sergeants. The British could stand it no more. They handed over responsibility to the newly formed United Nations.

In an important historical move, the Americans backed the Zionists. President Harry S. Truman was both personally sympathetic to the Jewish cause and anxious to secure the Jewish vote in the 1948 presidential election. On November 29, the United Nations General Assembly, with both Russian and American support, agreed that Palestine should be partitioned into a Jewish and an Arab state and that Jerusalem should be an international zone. Zionists accepted the principle of partition, but Arabs did not, reasoning that partition would deny them their "national rights" over the whole land, as they claimed was guaranteed by the UN charter. Immediately, the Arabs began to attack the Jewish settlements, but, under the leadership of David ben Gurion (1886–1973), the Jews consolidated their position.

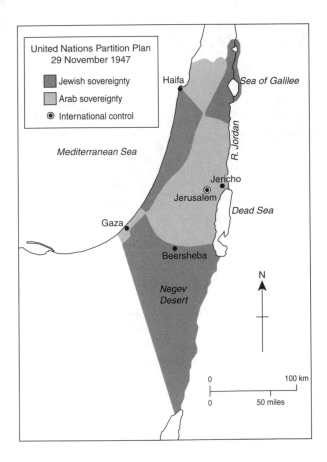

The State of Israel was proclaimed in 1948 after British withdrawal. In the face of Arab opposition, the United Nations had drawn up a plan whereby Palestine was to be divided into a Jewish state, an Arab state, and a small internationally administered zone around Jerusalem.

Independence Day

On May 14, 1948, the independence of the Jewish State of Palestine was declared, based both on the resolution of the United Nations and on "national and intrinsic right." The new nation was to be called Israel. Still the conflict continued, and by 1949 the Israelis held large tracts of land beyond the frontiers designated by the United Nations. An armistice was eventually signed between Israel on the one side and Jordan, Syria, Egypt, and Lebanon on the other. The peace was to be permanent.

However, war broke out again in 1956, in 1967 (when the Israelis captured Jerusalem and the West Bank of the Jordan, the Gaza Strip, and the Golan Heights), and in 1973. Even today, the problem of Palestinian refugees, who contributed most of the pre-war Arab population of Palestine, has still not been solved (and, in fact, things at the time of this publication seem to be getting much worse). In the 1947–1948 war, more than half a million Arab refugees fled from their homes. Some found sanctuary in the surrounding countries, but too many live in temporary camps that are a constant source of discontent and guerilla activity.

Trial and Error

In 1982, Israeli forces invaded Lebanon in order to destroy Arab guerilla bases that were threatening to the State of Israel. Five years later, Palestinians in the occupied territories began a grassroots, concentrated program of resistance (*intifada*), which involved stone throwing, ambushes, and selective strikes. Unable to quell the violence, Israelis realized that compromises would have to be made.

Beginning in 1991, further peace talks took place between the government and the Palestinian Liberation Organization (PLO), which raised hopes that an autonomous Arab Palestine could be created that would co-exist peaceably with Israel. Talks were interrupted, however, and the whole of Israeli society was rocked by the assassination of Prime Minister Rabin by an extremist Jewish student in 1995.

After 9/11 ...

In the final few years of the twentieth century, many attempts were made between Israel and Palestine to stop the violence and constant fighting. Despite the turmoil, Israeli prime minister Benjamin Netanyahu and PLO leader Yasir Arafat, as well as U.S. president Bill Clinton, who frequently attempted to act as a mediator, forged onward to try to find a resolution to the problems that plagued the area. However, the dawning of the twenty-first century was not to see this.

Did You Know?

Benjamin Netanyahu was the youngest prime minister elected in the history of the State of Israel.

Netanyahu served as prime minister until 1999, when Ariel Sharon defeated him in the next election, and the following year, George W. Bush was elected President of the United States. Both men have met with a challenge that neither could have predicted. On the beautiful, clear-skied morning of Tuesday, September 11, 2001, members of the extremist Islamic terrorist organization al-Qaeda flew two jets into each of the World Trade Center towers in New York City, as well as another into the Pentagon, and a fourth that crashed in Pennsylvania before it could hit its target, likely the White House. Thousands of innocent people were killed, and the feeling of safety that many Americans long took for granted was shaken to the core. Al-Qaeda's leader, Osama bin Laden, was quoted in a post-September 11 interview saying, "I tell Muslims to believe in the victory of God and in Jihad against the infidels of the world. The killing of Jews and Americans is one of the greatest duties."

Following the September 11 tragedy, relations between Israel and Palestine have become the worst they've ever been, and the State of Israel is in the throes of a new and perhaps ever-more frightening state of alarm. Terrorist bombings have become an every-day occurrence. Meanwhile, the threats of al-Qaeda against the United States, Israel, and any supporters of either continue to come.

It is difficult to say what will happen in Israel and the surrounding states. Much damage has been done and heels have been dug into the ground. There are times when it seems irresolvable. But there is one thing the people of Israel have miraculously maintained through their long and arduous history— faith—a strength that can be mightier than bombs.

The Least You Need to Know

- Adolf Hitler's vision and subsequent Nazi Holocaust killed six million Jews and went down in history as one of the most despicable atrocities committed against humankind.

- After World War II ended and the Holocaust was over, the State of Israel was established for the displaced European Jews.

- The struggle between displaced Jews going to their Promised Land and the displaced Palestinians of the area has long caused violence between Israel and Palestine.

- The events of September 11 brought about a whole new and frightening chapter in Israel's struggle to live in peace among the Arab nations.

Chapter 7

Judaism in the United States

In This Chapter

- The Jewish community in the United States
- Jews in U.S. business, commerce, and politics
- Are American Jews blending in or blending out?

We've noted it before and we'll note it again: The United States has the largest and most thriving Jewish population of any country, including Israel. Many Jews from all over the world consider the United States, melting pot that it is, as the most tolerant and fertile ground to establish a home. Of course, this does not mean that America is without anti-Semitism, racism, and a bunch of other isms, but that's inevitably what happens when there are a whole lot of different folks living together and trying to get along. Still, the American Jewish community is alive and well. Let's look at it a little closer.

United We Stand, Divided We Grow

Despite the many different sects of Judaism flourishing in the United States—from strict Orthodox to the liberal Reform to the pamphlet-handing Jews for Jesus—the United States remains the home of the largest, richest, and most powerful Jewish community in the world. It may come as a surprise to you that it is almost twice as large as that of the State of Israel, which comes second in size. Unlike the United States, where Ashkenazi Jews are prominent, Israeli society is approximately half Ashkenazi and half Sephardi. (See Chapter 4 for more on this.) Third in line for largest Jewish population are the combined states of the former Soviet Union. In these states, however, Jews were denied knowledge of their religious and cultural heritage during the years of the Communist Regime. The early twentieth century marked the growth in U.S. settlement as Shtetls slowly began to erode and America became the destination of choice. The United States offered new opportunities to these Eastern European Jews. It is estimated that between 1840 and 1925 more than 2.5 million people of Jewish origin entered the United States as immigrants.

Thriving in the Diaspora

Despite thriving Jewish communities worldwide, the best example of the fullness and diversity of Jewish life in the Dispersion is in the United States. Although not many families have been in the United States for more than three or four generations (and, as in Israel, their forebears come from all over the world), the influence of Jews in the Great American Melting Pot is undeniable.

The variety of institutions is astounding. There are synagogues representing every shade of religious and social opinion, including prayer groups for feminists and homosexuals. There is the whole spectrum of generous Jewish charities, liberally performing mitzvahs and supporting good causes in their communities and throughout the world at large.

In every major American city there are Jewish retirement homes and blocks of sheltered housing for the elderly and handicapped. There is a Jewish Family Agency, Jewish hospitals, and a Jewish burial society. The community supports innumerable educational establishments, varying from strictly Orthodox Yeshivot to Progressive Jewish day schools, from synagogue nurseries to kosher summer camps. For young adults there are Jewish Community Centers offering a wide range of leisure activities, Jewish country clubs, libraries, museums, and extensive programs of adult education.

Assimilation and the Long-Term Future

The American Jewish community remains the largest in the world and is more powerful than ever before. The days of private clubs and certain housing areas being closed to Jews are over. From the early 1960s,

Jewish young people have been moving in unprecedented numbers into the more prestigious universities and professional positions. Their progress has been astonishing.

By 1970, a quarter of the undergraduates at Harvard University were of Jewish origin, as were 40 percent of those at Columbia. This generation of students grew up to have considerable influence in the legal and political circles of the 1990s. President Clinton (1946–) appointed two Jews to the Supreme Court during his first administration, and two Jewish senators were elected to Congress in 1992. Al Gore chose Joseph Lieberman, a Jewish Senator from Connecticut, as his Democratic running mate in the 2000 Presidential elections, and Jews were represented in both houses in a proportion five times greater than their proportion in the population as a whole. It is the same story in medicine, in academia, in the entertainment industry, in journalism, in banking, and in the business world.

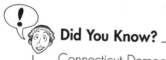 **Did You Know?**

Connecticut Democratic Senator Joseph Lieberman was chosen by Al Gore as his running mate in the 2000 presidential election, making him the first Jewish American to be nominated for that office. He also received more votes for vice president than any Democrat in history.

By 1994, American Jews formed less than 2 percent of the U.S. population, but they exerted influence in almost every public sphere. The community was overwhelmingly suburban, middle class, college-educated, and affluent. Significantly, from being traditionally liberal in politics, many became Republican in the Reagan/Bush era although the vast majority voted for the Democrat Bill Clinton both times that he ran for office. In recent years, perhaps, things have been less rosy for the young as programs of positive ethnic and sexual discrimination (i.e., giving a leg up to nonwhite males) have been disadvantageous to Jewish male students (but, happily, not to their sisters). Still, there is no evidence that the generation who grew up in the 1990s had greater difficulty reaching the upper echelons of American society, and at present, the Jewish community appears to be doing very well.

This is not to say that anti-Semitism no longer exists in the United States, but there is little evidence of it in polite society. Through educational programs, Holocaust memorials and museums, and in the artifacts of popular culture, the Holocaust illustrates all too clearly where Jew-hatred can lead. The Nazi period and subsequent anti-Semitism is still successfully kept in the public eye. Films such as *Sophie's Choice*, *Schindler's List*, and *Focus* (based on Arthur Miller's only novel) ensure that the suffering of the Jews is not forgotten.

Did You Know?

Schindler's List, a movie based on the true-life decision of German entrepreneur Oskar Schindler to rescue more than 1,100 Jews during the Nazi Holocaust, won seven Academy Awards® and has gone down in film history as one of the most honored films of all time.

The Anti-Defamation League, an organization founded to combat manifestations of anti-Semitism, has been particularly effective in combating the expression of anti-Jewish prejudice.

With the diminution of anti-Semitism, intermarriage between Jew and non-Jew becomes more common. Between 1900 and 1940, less than 3 percent of the married Jews were wedded to Gentile partners. The figure rose to 6.7 percent for those who married in the 1940s and 1950s. By 1970, the figure had leapt to 31.7 percent, and from the mid-1980s, it reached 52 percent. In other words, for every married Jewish couple, there are two mixed couples. In the past, Jewish men were far more likely to marry out of their faith than Jewish women. Often, however, these Gentile women were willing to convert to Judaism.

The Word

ADL (the Anti-Defamation League). The ADL is an organization that began in 1913 and still exists today to fight anti-Semitism and bigotry in the United States and abroad. Its national headquarters are in New York City, but there is a network of regional and satellite offices throughout America, and in Jerusalem, Vienna, and Moscow.

Today, though, only one in three spouses converts and less than one in three children of these mixed marriages is raised as a Jew. (Although, many aren't raised as Christians either. Many modern-day couples choose to raise their children with no organized religion at all.) It's a bit of a catch-22—as Jews become more and more blended into Gentile society, the adherence to Jewish law and tradition dwindles. In view of all this, many commentators believe that American Jews are, in the words of historian Norman Cantor, "on a one-way ticket to disappearance as a distinctive ethnic group."

However, the *seder* (the Passover meal) is an interesting example of how the face of the Jewish community may be changing in different ways. The less Orthodox may have a family meal that will involve saying the blessings and singing traditional songs, but everyone—men, women, and children alike—will join in as opposed to only the men in

Orthodox fashion. In other families there is little obvious religious observance, but the traditional Sabbath of Friday evening and Saturday are still regarded as special "home" time.

The Word

Seder. The traditional meal served during Passover.

Still, despite the worry among some of the Jewish community that American Jews are losing their "Jewishness," it is undeniable that the Jewish community in America is one that is thriving and growing, and certainly not about to abandon its Jewish identity.

The Least You Need to Know

- The American Jewish community remains the largest in the world—even to that of Israel.

- Jewish Americans have thrived in the United States, climbing the upper echelons of society and succeeding brilliantly.

- Although many young Jews marry outside the faith, the Jewish identity in America remains strong.

Chapter 8

Hope for the Future: Waiting for the Messiah

In This Chapter

- Unwavering support: the tenacity of the Orthodox in waiting for the Messiah
- Were Jews too quick to establish the Holy Land or has the golden age actually begun?
- How modern life and all its trappings make the question of the Messiah's arrival ever-more tenuous

One of the greatest challenges of faith is sustaining beyond science, logic, and doubt that what you can't see, hear, or touch is indeed real and worth all of your efforts. It would be difficult to argue that those who follow the Jewish belief that the *Messiah* is still to come don't have their work cut out for them. And yet, thousands of years later, the belief survives and Judaism remains a strong religious presence worldwide. Yet the challenges of the twenty-first century have set up a whole new set of hurdles for those of the Jewish faith. In this chapter, we look at the struggle in Judaism to maintain faith in the Messiah, and the modern challenges Jews face in holding onto this ideal.

The Word

Messiah. God's chosen King, who will establish his Kingdom on Earth and usher in a Golden Age of peace and harmony.

Waiting on a Friend

The strictly Orthodox inarguably maintain the most unwavering faith that the Messiah will arrive. Through the long centuries of exile from the Promised Land, the Jewish people hoped and prayed for signs that God would intervene in world history by sending his anointed king, the Messiah. According to the psalmist in the Bible, God promised that King David and his descendants would rule over Israel for all time. The last Davidic King was removed from the throne by the Babylonians in 586 B.C.E. (see Chapter 3 for more on the history of the Jewish faith). As the years passed and no Messiah came, God's pledge was seen as a prediction of the future.

Testament

Belief in the future Messiah was the twelfth of Maimonides' principles of the faith, and the philosopher insisted that anyone who has doubts about the Messiah contradicts the Torah.

In the long course of Jewish history, there have been many messianic claimants. The best known are Jesus of Nazareth (first century C.E.), the founder of Christianity, Simeon bar Kokhba (second century C.E.), who led a rebellion against the Romans in 132 C.E., David Alroy (twelfth century C.E.), who led the Jews of Baghdad to believe that they would all fly to Jerusalem on the wings of angels, and Shabbetai Zevi (1626–1676), who we discussed in Chapter 4. An important messianic candidate has also appeared in recent years. Menahem Mendel Schneersohn (1902–1994), the leader of the Lubavitcher Hasidim, was believed by his followers to fulfill the messianic prophecies. Despite the fervor of those devoted to him, though, the vast majority of Jews—Orthodox, Reform, and secular alike—reject this claim.

Did You Know?

Even after his death, many of the devoted disciples of Menahem Mendel Schneersohn were convinced that he would return again.

What Will Be, Will Be

Of course, as the years go by and a messiah who all Jews agree is the true one has not arrived, there has been much discussion as to what will happen when he does show up. There are, of course, a few different takes on this.

The rabbis of the Talmud believed that the Messiah will usher in a golden age, a time of total happiness. As God's chosen agent, he would restore justice, teach the Torah, and right all wrongs. The Twelve Tribes of the Israelite people would miraculously be gathered together again in the Land of Israel and all nations would look to Jerusalem for spiritual enlightenment.

This, of course, makes the Zionist movement (those who went to and settled in the Holy Land before the coming of the Messiah) a bit of a sticking point for the strictly Orthodox. According to the traditional scheme of things, the Jews were not meant to return to the land before the coming of the Messiah. In effect, the Zionists were presumptuous on the promise of the return and saw the establishment of the Jewish State as a political rather than a religious goal. In fact, there are still a few very Orthodox groups who do not accept the legitimacy of the State of Israel. Some may even live in the land, but they take no part in the political process. They continue to wait for divine deliverance. The majority of the Orthodox community, however, perceives the new State as the start of the fulfillment of the messianic age, but they believe it won't be complete until the Messiah's presence is known. In view of the current state of affairs in the Middle East, this position becomes increasingly difficult to sustain because a major characteristic of the days of the Messiah is universal peace—which is particularly lacking at this point in time.

The Reform Take on Divine Deliverance

At the other end of the religious spectrum, the leaders of the Reform movement in the nineteenth century also rejected the messianic hope, but for different reasons. They insisted that the Jews were not a nation but a religious community, and they considered the idea of the Messiah as too narrow. Instead, they understood the messianic age as a time of truth, justice, and peace that would be achieved by education, economic reform, and scientific discovery. It was the Holocaust, though, that finally convinced the Reform establishment of the merits of the Zionist cause.

Reform congregations are committed to social action as the divinely ordained means of transforming the world. In this century, Reform lawyers have been in the forefront of the civil rights cause; they have thrown their weight behind the liberation of women, and they have been closely involved in the various peace movements. Thus, the old expectation of God establishing his kingdom has been transformed into a secular commitment of social, political, and educational reform to be more in step with modern life.

Dawn of the Dead?

By the twelfth century, a belief in the final resurrection of the dead became an accepted take on what would happen during the Messianic Age. It was so established that it is listed as one of Maimonides' principles of the Jewish faith. The idea, as taught by the rabbis of the Talmud, was that in the Messianic Age, the dead would rise from their sleep and would be judged before God. Maimonides himself thought that after the resurrection, those who had been judged would die again, and it was only the souls of human beings that were immortal.

Traditionally, the Jewish hope for the future was centered on *this* world and not an afterlife. It is thought that the King-Messiah would establish God's kingdom on Earth (the Holy Land), and all wrongs would be righted. If this did not occur in one's own lifetime, it would happen in the days of one's children or one's children's children. This doctrine of personal immortality only began to develop in the fourth or third century B.C.E., possibly as a result of Babylonian influence. It wasn't (and hasn't by any means been) accepted by everyone. The modern understanding of scientific matter makes a physical resurrection difficult to accept.

Nonetheless, it is true that belief in a final reward and punishment is an integral part of the Jewish tradition. In the past, it was generally agreed that the righteous would enter Heaven, which is described in the literature as being a place of beauty and delight. Meanwhile, those who have been rejected by God will get their due and be subject to a series of appalling tortures. In fact, the notion of divine judgment is an essential component of the liturgy for the New Year and the Day of Atonement. However, modern Jews have, in general, rejected the idea of divine punishment. The notion of the evil-doers of the world not being punished at all and, in the end, finding divine reward is, however, a bit of a jagged pill to swallow. For many Jews, this theory makes it difficult to recognize the ulti-mate justice of God.

Israel: Promised Land or Political Stand?

It's easy for all parties to accept that modern Israel, the Jewish State, was not created by the Messiah. It was the result of massive Jewish immigration, sym-pathetic world opinion, and a resolution of the United Nations. But from its earliest days, it has been in peril. When the United Nations recom-mended in 1947 that there should be a Jewish State, the surrounding Arab nations were determined that it should not be in their territory in the Middle East. In effect, Israel was under siege (and continually seems to be so). In retribution, Israelis fought back and fought hard, and the War of Independence, as it came to be called, began. In the War of Indepen-dence, the Jewish settlers were fighting against a vastly larger force, and even when the Arabs were defeated, they refused to recognize the new State's existence. During that period, though, it seemed world opinion turned against Israel. In 1975, the United Nations condemned Zionism as a form of racism, and the Israeli army was increasingly seen as an oppressive, imperialistic force.

 Testament

> Between the end of the War of Independence in 1948 and 1993, more than 18,000 Israelis were killed in battle or were victims of terrorist attacks.

The Palestinian problem is far from being resolved at this point. After the Six Day War of 1967, the Israelis occupied the West Bank of the Jordan River and Gaza. These areas were the homes of millions of Arabs, refugees from the Israeli War of Independence, most of whom lived in poor housing and had few educational opportunities. New Jewish immigrants were encouraged to settle in those territories. In 1982, the army tried to root out the Palestinian terrorists once and for all by attacking their bases in Lebanon. This campaign did nothing to restore Israel's image in the eyes of the world, particularly after the inhabitants of a Muslim refugee camp were massacred by Lebanese Christian soldiers in alliance with Israel. Meanwhile, the Arabs living in the occupied territories responded by becoming more and more militant. The Arab Intifada (popular insurrection), which began in 1987, was difficult to control. Even the most Israel-loving Dispersion Jew was disturbed by pictures of Israeli soldiers firing at children throwing stones.

In 1993, the then Israeli Prime Minister, Yitzhak
Rabin (1922–1996), himself a military hero, symbol-
ically shook hands with Yassir Arafat (1929–), the
leader of the Palestinian Liberation Organization
(PLO). Both sides committed themselves to the
Oslo Accords, which included the idea of Palestinian
autonomy over Gaza and areas of the West Bank.
The PLO recognized Israel and Israel recognized
the right of the PLO to represent the Palestinians.

At this point, Israel was in need of economic and
political stability—for too long the country had been
dependent on American support. With the advent
of democracy in Russia, thousands of Russian Jews
were exerting their right under the Israeli Law of
Return to emigrate to Israel. Many of these people
were highly educated. It was becoming increasingly
necessary to develop an economy that could make
use of their technological expertise and support this
influx of new immigrants. If Israel was to establish
its own identity as an independent, economically
stable country, peace was a necessity.

 Did You Know? _____

> In the early 1990s, 10 percent of the
> Israeli population was unemployed.

The ultra-Orthodox in Israel are determined to
establish a "Greater Israel" based on the boundaries promised by God in the Bible. Meanwhile,

people of Arab origin who have Israeli residence and Israeli citizenship comprise at least 20 percent of Israel's population. However, the majority are regarded as second-class citizens by their Jewish neighbors, and they are underrepresented in the universities and the professions, adding to the difficulty in stabilizing the area.

But Will Unity Help or Hurt Israel?

Many of the surrounding Arab countries see peace with Israel as the first step in creating a regional economic common market. On both sides, there is an enormous incentive to establish a common trading alliance. For this to be successful, both Jewish and Muslim extremists will have to be sidelined—which, at this point in time, seems the most difficult of challenges.

This creates a different problem for Jews, though. When the day comes that Israelis are cooperating with the Jordanians, Syrians, and Lebanese on economic projects, will that social interaction lead to a melding of ethnicities and religions? At present, marriage is a problem in the Jewish State for anyone who cannot demonstrate a clear Jewish maternal line (see Chapter 1). Many of the Russian, Ethiopian, and American Reform immigrants have great difficulty in this regard. Marriage continues to be controlled by the Orthodox establishment who will only authorize marriages of one Jew (by their matrilineal definition) to another. Already this is the cause of much discontent. It stands to reason that it will get worse once there are Israeli/Arab economic ventures because Jewish/Muslim marriages are likely to follow. In the same way as young Jews in the Dispersion are increasingly choosing their spouses from among the Gentiles with whom they have grown up and been educated, the same trend may well occur in Israel in the future.

So what does this mean for Israel as the Promised Land? Will it become just one nation among many in the Middle East? Or will the difficulties between Islamic and Jewish residents continue to become more and more at odds? The strictly Orthodox will likely continue to inhabit their own self-imposed ghetto, but, despite their prolific birthrate, they will be only a small minority in the population. The vast majority will be secular Middle Easterners, descendants of both Jews and Arabs, dedicated not to the Torah and Talmud, but to prosperity and technological progress. It may be that the Ortho-dox will turn out to have been right after all— perhaps it is impossible to establish a Jewish State without the advent of God's Messiah.

I Am Woman! Judaism and Feminism

There is another, even more serious challenge to the traditional Jewish faith; it comes from the changing role of women in the world today.

Strict Orthodox Judaism is essentially a patriarchal religion in which men and women have clearly de-fined roles. Of course, you can argue that Jewishness itself is passed down from mother to child, giving women a vital role in Judaism, but the child itself is always described as a son or daughter of the father and not the mother.

Women are exempt from all time-bound positive commandments, so they are not expected to take an active part in the liturgical life of the synagogue. Their presence does not even count toward the necessary quorum for worship.

Did You Know? _____

If a woman's parents die and she has no brothers in the stricter sects of Judaism, she must either ask her husband or pay some other pious Jewish man to say Kaddish, the traditional prayer of mourning, for the deceased, as she is not allowed to do so herself.

Marriage and motherhood are the only acceptable destiny for a strict Orthodox girl. There is no parallel to the Christian monastic tradition where a particularly pious, talented, or intellectual young woman can develop her own interests and cultivate a personal relationship with the Almighty. In fact, in the 16 volumes of the *Encyclopaedia Judaica*, there are remarkably few entries for women. Only three books in the Hebrew Bible are named after

women—Ruth, Esther, and Judith. In general,
women are only remembered as the wives or moth-
ers of male heroes or scholars. According to the
Book of Genesis, woman was created to be a "help-
meet" for man. This has been understood to mean
that the wife was to free her husband from all
domestic cares so he was able to immerse himself
in Talmudic scholarship.

Little has changed in today's strict Orthodox communities of Europe, the United States, and Israel.
The strictly Orthodox have dealt with the challenge from the feminist movement by ignoring it.
In the State of Israel, because the Orthodox have
complete control in matters of personal status,
women continue to find themselves with certain
civil disabilities. Most acute is in the matter of
divorce. There is no civil divorce and, according to
Jewish law, divorce can only be given by a man to
a woman, not the other way around. However, in
other respects, women are not bound by Orthodox
law. The constitution of Israel guarantees the complete equality of men and women. Among the vast
majority of the Israeli population, daughters and
sons receive the same education and enjoy the same
professional opportunities. Thus, in the State of
Israel, secular Jewish women find themselves in a
strange position. On the one hand, they suffer a
huge civil disadvantage in the matter of divorce,
but in normal, everyday life, they can expect equality of treatment with their male colleagues.

> **Did You Know?**
>
> If a man refuses to divorce his wife, she has no legal redress in Orthodoxy. She may find herself tied to a wife beater, a child molester, or a mass murderer, but if he will not give her the necessary document, she cannot legally be free of him.

In the Dispersion, things are different. The vast majority of Jews are not affiliated with the strictly Orthodox. In Modern Orthodox synagogues, women can and do assume positions of leadership. They are synagogue presidents and leading fundraisers. Nonetheless, it is impossible for them to be ordained as rabbis, and they are not even counted among the necessary quorum for worship. This is because the Modern Orthodox believe that both the written and oral law were directly given by God and, therefore, cannot be changed in any way.

Things are very different in Conservative and Reform synagogues, however. There, the women and men sit together, and everyone takes full part in the service. Since the early 1970s, the Reform movement has ordained women as rabbis and, more recently, the Conservatives and Reconstructionists have followed suit.

Modern Jewry has been strongly influenced by the feminist movement; indeed many of the best-known feminist leaders are themselves of Jewish origin (who, at this point, hasn't heard of Gloria Steinam?). Among the non-Orthodox and secular Jews, the traditional passion for Talmudic study has been transformed into a desire that their children should enjoy the very best secular education that the Gentile world can offer. They want this for their daughters just as much as for their sons. Today there are large numbers of Jewish young women studying medicine or law, or who are attending business school. Among this highly educated group, late marriage is the norm. In fact, many choose never to get married at all and, even if they do marry, they are most unlikely to have more than two children. The birthrate among non-Orthodox Jewish couples is low, way below the basic regenerating level.

Did You Know?

The average number of children per Jewish family has dropped below the 2.3 per family average needed to sustain the current Jewish population.

Despite the efforts of the Modern Orthodox and the non-Orthodox synagogues, many of these clever, high-earning young women do not seem to be attracted to what Judaism has to offer. Even if they find a Jewish man to marry and they raise Jewish children, it is probable that their connection with the religious community will be tenuous at best. They will move easily in mainstream Gentile society, and it is likely that many of their friends will be non-Jews. For young people brought up with and educated among Gentile elite, intermarriage and complete assimilation is an ever-present likelihood.

Meanwhile, the strictly Orthodox, who do seem largely immune to the effects of secularization, practically barricade themselves into their own observant ghetto. They are the only members of the community who are producing large numbers of Jewish children. Even though the world of Orthodox Yeshivot and girls' seminaries has never been so thriving, the strictly Orthodox are cooperating less and less with the rest of the Jewish world, which they see as irredeemably assimilated and a threat to Judaism in general.

As such, many observers believe that there are no grounds for optimism. The birthrate of Jews in the Dispersion is too low, and the attractions of assimilation are too great. Admittedly, Israel will remain in the hands of the people who are descended from Jews, but increasingly some commentators believe that in future decades they, too, will intermarry with the surrounding nations and will perceive themselves as Israelis rather than as Jews. The only survivors will be the strictly Orthodox, who will continue to worship the God of their ancestors as their parents did before them, but they will be increasingly isolated from modern civilization. So, some wonder, when the Messiah does come, what will he find? Who will the Chosen People be at that point—a flock of loyal followers of the Torah or an amalgam of people comprised of mixed races and religions?

The Future and the Messiah

The Jewish belief in the future is obscure. The strictly Orthodox continue to pray that God will send his Messiah to bring the final golden age, to gather the remnants of the Jewish people, to resurrect the dead, and to exercise final judgment. However, the vast majority of Jewish people no longer expect this. The Reform and the Conservative Jews believe that the soul is immortal, but they are not precise in their teaching. In particular, they have rejected the idea of eternal torment and many go still further. Many do not expect God ever to make his presence manifest in the world, and they have lost all belief in personal immortality. The focus of their Jewishness lies either in their loyalty to the political State of Israel or in an abstract commitment to the survival of the Jewish people. These have become the twin pillars of modern Judaism— Israel and Jewish continuity.

The Least You Need to Know

- Orthodox Jews still wait for the coming of the Messiah and see much of modern life as a blasphemous threat to the golden age.

- Many modern Jews no longer believe that the Messiah will actually come, but that the golden age must be ushered in with science, progress, and human-interest endeavors.

- Feminism and intermarriage bring up more difficult questions for the future of the Jewish community and, in turn, make some wonder who the Chosen People will be in the future.

Chapter 9

Get a Life: Judaism from Birth to Death

In This Chapter

- The rite of circumcision
- The importance of bar and bat mitzvahs, education after the mitzvah, and how mitzvahs can differ for male and female children
- What the marriage ceremony is like
- Death rites—a celebration of life

Religion often provides the framework in people's lives—a structure that gives needed boundaries and laws to live by. In this chapter, we look at life—from birth to death—in the Jewish faith.

Birth Milah

The birth of a son in the stricter groups of the Jewish faith is traditionally a matter of great celebration, marked by the ritual circumcision and possibly a Redemption of the Firstborn ceremony.

From ancient times, all Jewish boys have been circumcised. This rite (known as the Birth Milah) is so ancient that, according to the tradition, it dates back to the time of the Patriarch Abraham.

The Word

Circumcision. In the Jewish faith, a traditional rite performed on male children in which the foreskin of the penis is removed eight days after birth. It symbolizes inclusion into the Jewish religious community.

During this rite, the child is held firmly and the actual surgery is performed by a Mohel, a professional circumciser. This is a job that requires considerable training.

Just before it is done, the father of the child makes a blessing:

> "Blessed art Thou, O Lord our God, King of the Universe, who has sanctified us through Thy commandments and hast commanded us to make our sons enter the covenant of Abraham."

To this, those in attendance respond,

> "Even as this child has entered into the covenant, so may he enter into the Torah, the marriage canopy, and into good deeds."

The child is given his Hebrew name, and the ceremony is generally followed by a party. The practice
of circumcision is deeply rooted in the community.
Secular Jews, too, will often circumcise their sons—
although perhaps by a surgeon instead of by a Mohel
at a religious ceremony. If the baby boy is the first
born of his mother, a further ceremony (Pidyan
Ha-Ben) takes place a month later. According to
the tradition, the firstborn son belongs to God and
must be redeemed by his parents. This involves the
symbolic payment of a sum of money or a small
article of silver to a priest.

Testament _____

Priests (or *kohens*) have few functions in
Judaism, but some members of the community, including Jews with the surname Cohen,
trace their ancestry to the priestly families
that served in ancient Israel.

At the ceremony, the father hands over the money
and the priest (kohen) holds it over the baby and
says, "This instead of that, this in commutation for
that and this in remission for that." He then prays
for the child and gives the traditional priestly bene-
diction. This ceremony is not practiced by Reform
Jews—partly because the Reform Jews are not convinced of claims of priestly ancestry, and second,
because it is seen as discriminatory to little girls.
And speaking of …

The birth of a daughter is marked only by a short blessing during the course of a normal synagogue service. To all those except the strictly adherent, this particular dividing of male and female children is thought of as a bit discriminatory because it makes it quite clear which gender is preferred by the Orthodox.

In recent years, largely as a result of the feminist movement, there have been attempts to introduce a special service for baby girls to celebrate their entry into the covenant. Although several alternatives have been proposed, few have as yet succeeded in capturing the potent mixture of pain, blood, insecurity, joy, and ancient symbolism of masculine circumcision.

All Grown Up

Reaching the age of maturity is yet another example of where the Orthodox make a clear line between men and women. When a boy reaches religious maturity at the age of 13, his bar mitzvah is a great event. In front of his extended family, his parents' friends, and the whole congregation, he is called up to read from the Torah scroll. For an Orthodox child who is experiencing an intensive Jewish education, this is not difficult. Boys raised in Orthodox households tend to find it easy to read the Hebrew text. Special lessons are available for the non-Orthodox to help those less familiar with the language so they can sing their "portions" with as much proficiency as their more observant fellows.

Often the bar mitzvah ceremony is accompanied by a lavish party. In general the religious establishment is embarrassed about this but feels powerless to stop it. Disappointingly, too, once the event is over, many boys feel no incentive to continue with their Jewish education.

There is no parallel service for girls in the tradition. It is recognized that girls mature earlier than boys, so a young Jewish woman has a bat mitzvah at the age of 12. Usually the occasion is marked only by a little party at home. However, in the Reform movement it is ensured that both boys and girls have their own ceremony. A girl's bat mitzvah is identical in every respect to a boy's bar mitzvah. Among the Modern Orthodox, girls also have a ceremony, but they do not read from the Torah scrolls. More than a mere concession—for Reform, Conservative, and Modern Orthodox alike—the bat mitzvah confirms contemporary views of Jewish women's roles in the community.

The Word

Bar/bat mitzvah. Translates into "son/daughter of the commandment." The coming-of-age ceremony in Judaism for boys (at age 13) and girls (at age 12).

Be True to Your School

Unfortunately, the discrimination between young men and women doesn't quite end here. The education of a boy is regarded as an important duty for parents from which no effort must be spared. The child must grow up learned in Torah and Talmud to be a credit to his family.

The education of a daughter, on the other hand, is a different matter for the Orthodox. It's important to them that a female be wise in the ways of running a kosher home, but traditionally she is not encouraged to be an intellectual. In many circles, women are not even permitted to study the Talmud. Although Orthodox communities in Israel and the United States do run religious schools for women, there are no women rabbis in the Orthodox community.

According to Jewish law, parents have an obligation to educate their children, and boys in particular are expected to be educated in Orthodox circles.

After the age of 13, the boy attains Jewish adulthood. From then on, he is expected to keep the commandments, and his presence in the synagogue counts toward the necessary quorum for worship.

Tying the Knot

In Orthodoxy, a Jewish wedding can be celebrated provided the particular synagogue accepts both partners as Jews (see Chapter 1). This takes place under a marriage canopy (a *chupah*) with both sets of parents supporting their children. A formal marriage contract (*ketubah*) is drawn up and signed by witnesses. Often these contracts are beautifully illustrated and are treasured as a keepsake by the couple.

Did You Know?

These days, increasing numbers of Jews enjoy customizing their own ketubah by incorporating artwork that reveals aspects of their two personalities. In this way they can create a uniquely personal item that affirms their faith in each other and in Judaism.

The bride and groom then drink from a glass of wine, and the bridegroom puts the wedding ring on the bride's finger saying the words: "Behold thou art betrothed to me with this ring in accordance with the Law of Moses and Israel."

This is followed by seven benedictions in which blessings are asked for the young couple, and the ceremony concludes with the bridegroom stepping on a glass and breaking it.

Testament

The origin of the custom of stepping on and breaking a glass during a Jewish wedding ceremony is obscure, but it is thought to be a reminder that even during the joy of a wedding, the destruction of Jerusalem must not be forgotten.

A Jewish wedding is the cause of tremendous rejoicing. To quote one of the blessings, marriage is regarded as a state of "Joy and gladness, laughter and exaltation, pleasure and delight, love, peace, and friendship."

Did You Know?

Judaism does not recognize divorce, as it is regarded as a tragedy. Thus, Jews are known for their strong family life.

The Final Chapter

When life comes to an end, the Jewish tradition emphasizes that the utmost regard and consideration should be shown to the dying. They should be urged to make their final confession to God, and ideally their last words will be those of the Shema ("Hear O Israel, the Lord our God, the Lord is One").

According to Jewish law, a body must be buried as soon as possible after death, and the general principle is that the dead must be honored. The body must never be left alone. Among the Orthodox, it is ritually washed and buried in a simple linen or cotton shroud, and the coffin contains no metal. The rabbi leads the funeral procession to the cemetery. Prayers are said while the coffin is lowered into the ground and the grave filled. Generally, a eulogy is made extolling the virtues of the deceased, and finally the Kaddish—a prayer praising God and for peace—is recited.

Once the funeral is over, the family returns home to begin a seven-day period of mourning. This is known as sitting Shiva. During this week, visitors from the community come to express their condolences, and the family does not leave the house except perhaps to go to synagogue. During this time, the mourners should recite the Kaddish three times each day to coincide with the daily services. Then, for the next 30 days, there is a time of lesser mourning when the Kaddish continues to be said, but the mourners gradually resume their regular routines. In the case of parents, Kaddish is said for a full year. Because it can only be said in a quorum of 10 men, attendance at synagogue is mandatory during this period. Subsequently, every year the dead person is remembered on the Hebrew date of his or her death. This death anniversary is known as the *Yahrzeit*, and the practice is to light a candle that burns for the full day. Thus, in the Jewish tradition the memory of those who have died is kept alive in the minds and hearts of those who loved them by a regular annual ritual.

The Word

Yahrzeit. After a person of the Jewish faith passes on, Yahrzeit is a ceremony observed one year after their death as a way of keeping alive the memory of the deceased. It also officially signifies the end of the mourning period.

By contrast with the Orthodox, Reform Jews occasionally choose to be cremated. Nonetheless, the practices of saying Kaddish occasionally and lighting a Yahrzeit candle are widely observed—even among the most secular.

The Least You Need to Know

- The Jewish life is marked by many important ceremonies and rites of passage.

- Male and female children can have very different lives depending on the strictness of the group their parents follow.

- Bar and bat mitzvah is the most important ceremony in a young person's life, as it marks their entry into adulthood.

- After a person of the Jewish faith passes on, he or she is remembered in a ceremony one year later to the day of death known as the Yahrzeit. It is a way of keeping alive the memory of the deceased.

Chapter 10

Tradition! Celebrations and Traditions in the Jewish Faith

In This Chapter

- The role of the Sabbath and the synagogue in Jewish life
- How dress and food play a large role in the lives of the strictly observant
- The three most important holidays on the Jewish Calendar: Passover, Shavuot, and Sukkot
- Other important dates—and how and why they're acknowledged

Traditions—everyone has some. The Jewish faith, however, is so full of beautiful, rich customs steeped in the long history from which they come and the new ways in which they are being celebrated. In this chapter, we delve into these customs and rituals, how they're celebrated, and how they originated.

Keep It Holy: The Sabbath

Genesis, the first book of the Hebrew bible, states that in the course of six days God made heaven and earth and created "Man in His image." But on the seventh day, He took a break. This has been known ever since as the *Sabbath*. It is said in the Bible that when Moses received the Ten Commandments on Mount Sinai, God commanded the Israelites, "Remember the Sabbath, and keep it holy."

The Word

Sabbath. In the Jewish faith, Saturday is the official day of rest. The Sabbath occurs from sundown Friday evening until sundown Saturday evening.

The Sabbath—which in the Jewish tradition begins on Friday evening and ends on Saturday evening—is considered the holiest day of the year (with the possible exception of Yom Kippur, the Day of Atonement), even though it occurs 52 times every 12 months. (Christians also acknowledge the notion of the Sabbath, but they celebrate it on Sundays.)

At Your Service: In the Synagogue

Services are held three times a day in Orthodox synagogues. This corresponds with the time the sacrifices were offered in the Temple in Jerusalem.

For the service to take place, there must be at least 10 adult men present. Women traditionally do not count toward this quorum. Non-Orthodox Jews, who insist on absolute equality between the sexes, count women in. Most Reform Jews (as they are called), however, do not hold daily services.

At the core of the liturgy are two prayers, the *Shema* ("Hear O Israel …") and the *Amidah*, originally a series of 18 blessings. The *Shema* declares the essential unity of God and the necessity of remembering His commandments; the Amidah is a series of 18 benedictions. The commandments are to be "bound as frontlets between your eyes and you shall write them on the doorposts of your house." Jews fulfill this by putting on *phylacteries* and by nailing a *mezuzah* to their doorposts.

In Orthodox Judaism, only men wear phylacteries, but in Reform Judaism, women, especially women rabbis, sometimes also wear them. Both the phylacteries and the mezuzah are visible signs that remind the pious of their duty toward God and make them recall their awesome obligations as members of the chosen people.

The blessings of the Amidah prayer are traditionally recited while standing and include a request for the restoration of the Temple. God is also thanked for His many mercies, and peace is asked for the people of Israel. In Reform Judaism, the prayer for peace is asked for Israel and the whole world. Other important prayers in the daily service include the *Kaddish* and the *Alenu*. The Kaddish is an expression of longing for the establishment of God's sovereignty over the Earth. It is said at the end of each major section of the liturgy and by mourners at the end of the service (it's a religious obligation to recite *Kaddish* for 11 months after the death of a close relative). The *Alenu* prayer proclaims the Kingship of God over all the world, and it concludes the service. Although the synagogue is the central communal institution of the Jewish faith, the home remains the real focus of religious life. Traditionally, women are exempt from the time-bound commandments, such as attending the daily services, because their role as homemaker and mother is considered a vital and time-consuming one.

The Word

Phylacteries. Two special boxes containing certain biblical verses written by hand on parchment that are attached to two straps. One box is placed over the head so it sits squarely between the eyes and the other is wound around the left arm so that it lies against the heart. They are worn during the morning service every day except the Sabbath and during festivals.

Mezuzah. A parchment scroll contained in a case. On the parchment is written the first two paragraphs of the Shema prayer. The box is nailed on the right-hand doorpost, usually on the front door. The strictly Orthodox, however, have one on every door in the house except the bathroom.

Ready to Wear: Dress

Among the Orthodox, every detail of daily life is covered by the commandments. This even includes food and clothing. One of the most recognizable signs of a male Jew is the skull cap, called yarmulke or *kippah*. The strictly Orthodox have it on at all times, but the Progressive tend to only wear it for prayer. You'd think this tradition would be an ancient one but, oddly, the custom only dates back to about the twelfth century C.E. (and was probably only introduced to distinguish Jews from Christians because Christian men always pray with their heads uncovered). Orthodox men also generally have beards. This is because the Book of Leviticus forbids the cutting of the corner of the facial hair. It is also customary to allow the side locks to grow.

Another element of Orthodox appearance is the wearing of fringes. According to the Torah, the Israelites were instructed to "make tassels on the corner of their garments … it shall be to you a tassel to look upon and to remember all the commandments." This is fulfilled by wearing an undergarment (*talit*) with fringes (*tzitzit*) on the four corners.

The Word

Fringes. Ritual tassels attached to the corners of garments.

For Modern Orthodox and Reform Jews, the talit is a prayer shawl worn as an overgarment. It is sometimes worn by women as well as men in Reform Judaism. The fringes of the talit are tied in a particular way to symbolize the numerical value of the name of God.

Because it is traditionally an undergarment, the talit is not normally seen, although it's not unheard of for the fringe to be brought out above the trouser waistband and tucked into a pocket. Similar fringes are put on the four corners of the shawl, which is worn for prayer in the synagogue. Orthodox women's dress is characterized by modesty. Married women are expected to keep their heads covered at all times and, particularly among the Hasidim, this is fulfilled by wearing a wig. In addition, men are not allowed to wear women's clothes nor women men's; this means that young Orthodox women are not to be seen wearing garments such as jeans.

Let's Eat: Food and the Jewish Faith

If there is a single factor that has distinguished the Jewish people from others, it's their food laws. Muslims inherited the idea of ritually pure food from the Jews, but most Christians by contrast regard the restrictions as unimportant because they believe the New Testament supersedes the Old.

Not only are certain categories of food completely forbidden, but even permitted animals and birds must be slaughtered in a particular way and milk foods must not be eaten with meat foods. This means, in effect, that all secular restaurant food and everything prepared in Gentile houses is non*kosher* (ritually unfit to eat).

The Word

Kosher. Food that is prepared according to the strict laws of the Kashrut and thus deemed ritually fit to eat.

According to the creation story in the book of Genesis, the first human beings were vegetarians. Meat eating was only permitted after the Great Flood. Only animals that have both a cloven hoof and chew the cud may be eaten, and only birds that are commonly used for food qualify. Pigs, for example, are forbidden because they do not chew the cud, and all birds of prey are nonkosher.

Did You Know?

Many authorities teach that when the Messiah comes, humanity will return to vegetarianism.

When eating animal foods, the creature must be slaughtered by a qualified butcher. It is killed by a quick downward slice to the throat and hung so that the blood is immediately drained. Eating the blood is not allowed. There are no specific rules of slaughter for fish, but not all sea creatures are permitted—only those with both fins and scales. Thus, observant Jews do no eat any form of shellfish or eel. In addition, in three places, the Pentateuch states, "You shall not seethe the kid in its mother's milk." Generally, this is interpreted to mean that meat and dairy food may not be eaten together.

Because minute particles of food can remain on crockery and cutlery, strictly observant households usually contain two completely different sets of plates and saucepans. There must even be separate washing bowls, draining boards, and preparation areas. Today, in strictly observant homes, it is not uncommon to see two sinks, two refrigerators, and even two dishwashers! It also means that no manufactured foods can enter the house unless they are guaranteed to be kosher—that the rules of slaughter have been observed and that there is not intermingling of milk and meat. Many mass-produced products today carry a certificate that confirms every stage of the processing has been inspected by a recognized religious authority.

There are different ways of observing the food laws, though, and not all households assume the strictest interpretation of them. For the very Orthodox, food is only kosher if it is approved by one of their own rabbinical authorities. Most Modern Orthodox, though, would accept any kosher authority, and some may make various compromises in their own lives. So, for example, they might keep a kosher home, but eat any vegetarian food when dining out—or they might eat anything if dining out. The laws of Kashrut are also increasingly being practiced by Conservatives and the Reform. Some keep kosher homes; some merely avoid pork and shellfish. Vegetarianism, both for religious and health reasons, appears to be on the increase. Many other Jews simply ignore the food laws, reasoning that they have no moral validity other than reminding people they are Jewish.

The laws of Kashrut, together with the laws for clothing and for every other aspect of Jewish daily life, are believed to have been laid down by God for His chosen people. That, for the Orthodox, is the end of the matter. Among the observant, Jewish living in every detail is a reminder of the special relationship that exists between God and Israel. It calls for no other justification of these traditions.

Day by Day: The Jewish Calendar

Traditionally, Jewish life is dominated by the regular rhythm of the weekly Sabbath and the annual fast days and festivals. Because the Jewish calendar year is based on a lunar calendar (secular calendars are solar-based), these yearly celebrations do not seem to occur on the same day every year. The 12 Jewish months contain only 354 days, and the shortfall is made up by adding a thirteenth month every few years. This ensures that the festivals occur at roughly the same time of year, although not on the same secular date.

According to the Book of Deuteronomy, the Jewish people are to celebrate three pilgrim festivals every year: "Three times a year all your males shall appear before the Lord your god at a place which He will choose: at the festival of unleavened bread (Passover), at the feast of Weeks (*Shavuot*), and at the feast of booths (*Sukkot*)." When the Temple was still standing, thousands of Jews went to Jerusalem to offer sacrifices on these days. All three feasts have agricultural connotations as well as commemorating events in Jewish history.

The Word

Passover, Shavuot, and Sukkot. The three Pilgrim festivals on the Jewish calendar—called this because they were traditionally celebrated in Jerusalem.

Liberation Day: Passover

Passover (Pesach), the spring festival, celebrates the start of the barley harvest, as well as the liberation of the Jews from slavery in Egypt. It lasts for seven days (eight outside the land of Israel), and during this time, observant Jews eat nothing made with raising agents, the whole house must be cleaned from top to bottom, and special Passover cutlery and crockery must be used.

On the first night, a special Passover meal (*seder*) is eaten during which the story of God's rescue of the Jews is told once more. Even the most secular attend a Passover meal because it's an opportunity for the whole extended family to get together. The evening always ends with the long-cherished hope, "Next year in Jerusalem!"

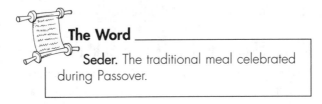

The Word

Seder. The traditional meal celebrated during Passover.

Unlike most festivals, which center on the synagogue, the highpoint of Passover, the seder meal, takes place at home. It is suffused with vividly contrasting symbols. Salt water (for tears) and horseradish (for bitterness) hark back to the days when Jews were slaves in Egypt. Yet the mandatory four cups of wine and copious cushions remind them that they are now free. As for eggs and fresh greens, these symbolize the hope of spring, rebirth, and fertility.

Harvest Moon: Shavuot

Shavuot celebrates the end of the barley harvest and occurs seven weeks after Passover. It also commemorates the giving of the Torah to Moses on Mount Sinai. In a sense, this holiday is the birthday of the Jewish religion. It is the custom to eat milk foods on Shavuot because, like milk, the Torah nourishes everyone from the very young to the very old, and traditionally, it is the time when boys and girls graduate from the synagogue religious school, having completed their formal religious education. Among the Reform, the ceremony of confirmation has been introduced for 16-year-olds as an incentive to stay in school beyond the bar/bat mitzvah age.

Where I Hang My Hat Is Home: Sukkot

Sukkot, the feast of tabernacles (temporary shelters), takes place in the autumn. It is a harvest festival as well as a reminder of the Jews' wanderings in the wilderness before they reached the Promised Land. They are supposed to live in a tabernacle (a temporary booth or hut) for the full eight (or nine outside Israel) days of the festival, and there are detailed specifications as to how the structure should be built. All main meals should be eaten there, but in colder climates there's no obligation to sleep in it. Jews are also instructed on how to make a *lulav*, a bundle of palm, willow, and myrtle branches. Holding this in one hand and a citron (or etrog, a lemonlike fruit) in the other, they wave the lulav in all directions in the synagogue to symbolize God's control of all space. On the final day, the annual cycle of Torah reading is ended and a new cycle is begun. Finally, the Torah scrolls are carried in procession around the synagogue amidst laughter and joy.

> **Did You Know?** _____
>
> In Hasidic communities, the enthusiasm is so great during the Torah scroll procession that it is not unusual for the celebration to spill out onto the street.

And the Celebrations Continue ...

There are also various minor and joyous festivals in the Jewish faith that are particularly popular with children—the two best known being Hanukkah, the feast of lights, and Purim, the feast of Esther.

In recent years, Hanukkah has become a much bigger deal than it used to be because it generally occurs at the same time as the Christian and commercial festival of Christmas. It celebrates the victory of Judas Maccabeus over the Hellenizing Selucid kings of the second century B.C.E. Hanukkah lasts for eight nights; presents are exchanged, and an additional candle is lit every night.

Purim occurs in the late winter and commemorates the escape of the Jewish people from the murderous designs of the wicked Haman. Haman, according to the biblical Book of Esther, wanted to destroy the Persian Jewish community. This festival is celebrated in the synagogue with readings and pageants.

The most important Jewish solemn days begin with the New Year (*Rosh Hashanah*) in the fall. This is the start of the Ten Days of Penitence, which conclude with the Day of Atonement (Yom Kippur). The Mishnah teaches that all human beings go before God on the New Year and are subject to judgment. A very small portion are seen to be fully righteous, and another group is immediately rejected as irredeemably wicked. (Don't panic, the vast majority are in the middle!) They have 10 days to repent of their evil ways and to purge themselves in the great fast of Yom Kippur. On Rosh Hashanah, the *shofar* (ram's horn) is blown. This makes a strange, unearthly sound that calls the people to repentance. As the great twelfth-century philosopher, Maimonides, put it, the shofar is commanding, "Awake you sinners and ponder your deeds; remember your Creator, forsake evil and return to God."

The Day of Atonement is the most solemn day in the Jewish year. Every adult Jew, male and female, is expected to fast from sunset until nightfall the next day to atone for their sins. The observant spend the whole day in synagogue praying for forgiveness. Even the more secular frequently attend the services on Rosh Hashanah and Yom Kippur.

Other fasts include the Ninth Day of Av (Tisha B'Av), which commemorates the destruction of the Temple by the Babylonians in 586 B.C.E., and by the Romans in 70 C.E.

Did You Know? _____

Reform Jews generally don't observe the Ninth Day of Av on the grounds that they neither expect nor desire the rebuilding of the Temple.

Less important are the fast of Tammuz, which commemorates the breaching of the walls of Jerusalem by the Babylonian and Roman armies, and the fast of Tevet, when the start of the Babylonian siege is remembered. In Israel, this is also observed as a day of remembrance for the six million Jews who died in the Nazi Holocaust. Elements of fasting include abstention from food and drink, from bathing, from making love, and from wearing leather.

In general, Judaism in not a particularly ascetic religion, but through this annual pattern of fasts, the pious Jew can discipline his physical nature and vicariously share in the disasters that have befallen the Jewish people through the ages.

The Least You Need to Know

- The Sabbath, the synagogue, and the home are central parts of observant Jewish life.
- According to the Torah, strict laws of dress and food preparation must be adhered to.
- The festivals of Passover, Shavuot, and Sukkot and the fasts of Rosh Hashanah and Yom Kippur are the most important on the Jewish lunar calendar.

Glossary

Agudut Israel   Orthodox organization set up to oppose Zionism.

amidah   Prayer consisting originally of 18 benedictions recited at the daily synagogue services.

anti-Semitism   Hatred of the Jews.

ark   Original container for the tablets of the law; a cupboard in the synagogue in which the Torah scrolls are kept.

Ashkenazim   Jews who settled in Northern France, Germany, and Eastern Europe, and their descendants in Israel and the United States.

assimilation   The loss of Jewish identity in mainstream Gentile culture.

Av 9   A fast commemorating the loss of the Jerusalem Temple.

bar mitzvah   The coming-of-age ceremony for a boy at the age of 13.

bat mitzvah   The coming-of-age ceremony for a girl at the age of 12.

B.C.E. Before the Common Era.

Blood Libel Accusation that Jews murder Christian children and use their blood in the making of Passover unleavened bread.

Canon The established books of scripture.

C.E. Common Era.

chief rabbi Established central religious authority of a particular Jewish community.

chosen people Jews believe that they were chosen by God to keep His Torah.

Conservatives A non-Orthodox movement within American Judaism.

covenant Special agreement between God and the Jewish people.

Crusades Medieval Christian movement to evict the Muslims from Palestine.

Day of Atonement Most holy day of the Jewish year that involves a day-long fast and prayers for forgiveness.

Dead Sea Scrolls Collection of ancient scrolls probably produced by the Essenes.

Dispersion The Jewish communities living outside Israel.

Enlightenment The secular scientific and educational revolution of the late eighteenth and early nineteenth centuries.

Essenes   Monastic communities of Jews who flourished in the first century C.E.

exegesis   Interpretation of sacred texts.

Exilarch   Head of the Babylonian Jewish community from the first to thirteenth centuries C.E.

fast   Day of abstention from food.

fringes (tzitzit)   Ritual tassels attached to the corners of garments.

gaon   Title of the heads of the Babylonian Talmudic academies.

Gentile   Non-Jew.

ghetto   Place set aside for Jewish residence.

Gospel   Christian story of the life and work of their chosen Messiah, Jesus Christ.

Hagaddah   The order of service of the Passover meal.

Halakhah   Jewish law.

Hanukkah   Winter festival celebrating the victory of the Maccabees over the Hellenizers.

Hasidim   Adherents of an eighteenth-century Eastern European Jewish mystical movement.

Hellenizers   Those who tried to introduce Greek ideas in the fourth century B.C.E.

High Priest   The Israelite Chief Priest who served in the Temple in Jerusalem.

Holocaust   The destruction of European Jewry by the Nazis between 1933 and 1945 during World War II.

Holy of Holies   The deepest sanctuary of the Jerusalem Temple.

humanistic Judaism   A radical movement within modern American Jewry that, among other things, doesn't hold believing in God as necessary to being Jewish.

intermarriage   Marriage between a Jew and a Gentile.

Israelites   The Jewish people, particularly in biblical times.

Kaddish   Prayer extolling God's greatness said by mourners.

Karaites   Adherents of a heretical sect of Judaism founded in the eight century C.E.

Kashrut   The laws governing food.

kibbutz   An Israeli agricultural collective.

kippah   Skull cap.

Knesset   The Israeli elected assembly.

kosher   Food that is fit to eat because it conforms to the laws of Kashrut.

Law of Return   The law that gives every Jew the right to settle in Israel.

lulav   Bundle of myrtle, palm, and willow branches that is used during the services on Sukkkot.

matrilineal   Descended from the mother.

Messiah   In Judaism, God's chosen King who will establish His Kingdom on Earth.

mezuzah   Parchment scroll attached to the doorposts of a Jewish house.

midrash   Rabbinic commentary on the Bible.

mikveh   Community ritual bath where women cleanse themselves after menstruation.

Mishnah   Oral law. Also the title of Judah ha-Nasi's second-century compilation of the oral law.

mitzvah   Commandment.

Mizrakhi   A party founded for Orthodox Zionists.

Modern Orthodox   Adherents of a modernist movement within Orthodoxy.

mohel   Ritual circumciser.

monotheists   Those who believe in one God.

Nasi   Title of the leader of the Palestinian Jewish community from the second to fourth centuries C.E.

New Testament   The concluding part of the Christian scripture describing the life of Jesus Christ and early church history.

New Year   First day of the month of Tishri, the start of the Ten Days of Penitence.

oral law   The oral interpretation of the written law, recorded in the Mishnah and Talmud.

Orthodox   Those who believe the written and oral law were given by God and must be obeyed in every particular.

Passover   Spring festival celebrating the liberation of the Jews from slavery in Egypt.

patriarchs   The forefathers of the Jewish people—Abraham, Isaac, and Jacob (Israel).

Pentateuch   The first five books of the Hebrew scriptures: Genesis, Exodus, Leviticus, Numbers, and Deuteronomy.

Pesah   Passover.

Pharisees   A religious sect of the Second Temple era who were scrupulous in obeying both written and oral law.

phylacteries (tefilin)   Boxes containing parchment scrolls that pious Jews bind each day on their arms and foreheads.

Pilgrim Festivals   Passover, Shavuot, and Sukkot, so called because they were traditionally celebrated in Jerusalem.

piyyutim   Poems that are used as prayers.

Poale Zion   A socialist movement within Zionism.

pogrom   An attack, often against the Jews, in nineteenth- and early twentieth-century Russia and Poland.

Progressive   Non-Orthodox Jew.

Promised Land   Israel; the land promised by God to Abraham and his descendants in the Bible.

prophet   One who speaks the word of God. The classical prophets are those whose words are preserved in the Bible.

proselyte   A convert.

Purim   Festival celebrating the deliverance of the Jews of Persia as recorded in the Book of Esther.

rabbi   A recognized Jewish teacher and spiritual leader.

Rabbinite   One who, in contrast to the Karaites, accepted the validity of the oral law.

rab/rav   Title given to Jewish teachers in Babylonia.

Reconstructionists   Adherents to a radical twentieth-century Jewish movement who regard Judaism as an evolving civilization.

Reform   A Progressive denomination that has attempted to make Judaism compatible with modern historical knowledge.

resurrection   The belief that the dead will rise from their graves to be judged by God.

Rosh Hashanah   The Jewish New Year.

Sabbath   Saturday, the day of rest. Begins at sundown Friday evening and ends at sundown Saturday evening.

Sadducees   Aristocratic priestly sect in the days of the Second Temple.

Samaritans   Descendants of the Northern and Southern Kingdom who intermarried with the surrounding peoples during the Babylonian empire.

Sanhedrin   Supreme religious assembly of the Jews at the time of the Second Temple and later.

scroll   Rolled length of parchment on which the Holy Books are written.

seder   Passover meal.

Selihot   Penitential prayers composed by the Ashkenazim.

Sephardim   Jews of Spanish or Asian origin.

Septuagint   Third-century B.C.E. Greek translation of the Hebrew scriptures.

Shabbat   Follower of the seventeenth-century false Messiah, Shabbetai Zevi.

Shabbos   The Sabbath.

Shavuot   Festival celebrating the giving of the Torah by God to Moses on Mt. Sinai.

Shema   The primary declaration of the Jewish faith.

Shiva   Seven-day period of mourning after the death of a close relative.

shofar   Ram's horn trumpet blown on Rosh Hashanah and Yom Kippur.

Shtetl   Eastern European village inhabited mainly by Jews.

Sukkot   Festival commemorating the Jews' wandering in the wilderness.

synagogue   House of worship.

tabernacles, feast of   Temporary shelters built during the festival of Sukkot.

talit   Undergarment with fringes (tzitzit) worn by Orthodox Jews.

Talmud   Compendium of oral law compiled in Palestine in the late fifth century and in Babylon in the early sixth century.

temple   Central shrine of ancient times; modern Reform synagogue.

Ten Commandments   Ten laws given to Moses as recorded in Exodus 20:2–14.

Ten Days of Penitence   Period from Rosh Hashanah to Yom Kippur.

Torah   God's revelation to the Jews; Jewish law; the Pentateuch.

Torah Scroll   Scroll on which the Pentateuch is written.

Tsaddik   Hereditary Hasidic leader.

Wall   Remaining part of the Jerusalem Temple.

Weeks, feast of   Shavuot.

World Zionist Organization   Central Zionist group.

written law   The laws of the Pentateuch.

yahrzeit   Anniversary of the death of a close relative.

yarmulke   Skull cap worn by Jewish men.

Yeshiva (pl. Yeshivot)   Talmudic academy.

Yiddish   Language of Eastern European Jewry.

Yom Kippur   Most important fast of the Jewish year.

Zealots   Jewish rebels against the Roman Empire.

Zionists   Those who are dedicated to restoring the Promised Land to the Jewish people.

Pronunciation Guide

This guide gives an accepted pronunciation of terms as simply as possible. Syllables are separated by a space, and those that are stressed are printed in italics. Letters are pronounced in the usual manner for English unless they are clarified in the following list:

a	fl*a*t
aa	f*a*ther
ai	th*e*re
ee	s*ee*
e	l*e*t
Ī	h*i*gh
ī	p*i*ty
ō	n*o*
o	n*o*t
oo	f*oo*d
yoo	y*ou*
u	b*u*t

ă	ab*o*ut
ch	*ch*urch
g	*g*ame
j	*j*et
kh	guttural aspiration (ch sound in Hebrew and German)
sh	*sh*ine
ts	car*ts*

Agudat Israel: ah goo *dat* iz raa ăl

amidah: ah mee *dah*

Ashkenazim: ahsh ke *nah* zeem

Av: *ahv*

bar mitzvah: bahr mits *vah*

bat mitzvah: baht mits *vah*

gaon: gai *ōn*

Gentile: jen *tīl*

Hagaddah: hah gah *dah*

Halakhah: hah lah *khah*

Hanukkah: hah na kăh

Hasidim: ha *sid* eem

Havdalah: hahv dah *lah*

Kaddish: kah *dish*

Kashrut: kahsh *root*

kibbutz: ki *boots*

kippah: kip *ah*

Knesset: *kne* set

kosher: *kō* sher

lulav: *loo* lahv

Maskilim: mah skee *leem*

mezuzah: me zoo *zah*

midrash: mi *drahsh*

Mishnah: mish *nah*

mitzvah: mits *vah*

Mizrachi: miz rah *khee*

mohel: *mō* *hel*

Nasi: *nah* see

Pentateuch: *pen* ta tyook

Pesah: *pe* sah

Pharisees: *far* i seez

phylacteries: fa *lak* ter eez

piyyutim: pee yoo *teem*

Poale Zion: po *al* e tsī *ōn*

Purim: poo *reem*

rabbi: r*a* bī

rav: *rahv*

Rosh Hashanah: *rōsh* hah shah *nah*

Sadducees: *sad* yoo seez

Selihot: să *lee* hōt

Sephardim: se fahr *deem*

Shabbatean: shah *baht* ee an

Shabbos: *shaa* bos

Shavuot: shah voo *ot*

Shema: shă *mah*

Shiva: *shee* vah

shofar: sho *fahr*

shtetl: *shtet* ăl

synagogue: *sin* ah gog

Talmud: tahl *mood*

Torah: tō *rah*

yahrzeit: *yahr* tsĭt

yarmulke: *yahr* mă l kă

Yeshiva: yă *shee* vah

Yom Kippur: *yōm* ki *poor*

Zealot: *zel* ă t

Festivals, Fasts, and Feasts by Season

Season	Date (Jewish Calendar)	Festival
Spring	Nisan 15–22	Passover—celebration of the liberation from slavery in Egypt.
	Iyyar 5	Israel Independence Day.
	Shivan 6–7	Shavuot—commemoration of the giving of the law to Moses on Mount Sinai.
Summer	Tammuz 17	Fast of Tammuz—remembering the breaching of the Jerusalem walls by Babylonians in 586 B.C.E. and 70 C.E.
	Av 9	Tishnah B'Av—mourning the destruction of the Jerusalem Temple in 586 B.C.E. and 70 C.E.

Season	Date (Jewish Calendar)	Festival
Autumn	Tishri 1–2	Rosh Hashanah—the New Year in which Jews are called to repentance.
	Tishri 10	Yom Kippur—the Day of Atonement. The day is dedicated to prayer and fasting to atone for sin.
	Tishri 15–21	Sukkot—the feast of tabernacles in which Jews live in booths to remember their ancestors' sojourn in the wilderness.
	Tishri 20–21	Simhat Torah—the Rejoicing in the law. The annual cycle of Torah readings concludes and begins anew.
Winter	Kislev 25–Tevet 3	Hanukkah—Festival of Lights, celebrating the defeat of the Hellenizing king by Judas Maccabeus.
	Tevet 10	Fast of Tevet—remembering the start of the Babylonian siege and the victims of the Nazi Holocaust.
	Adar 14	Purim—commemorating the foiling of plans to destroy Persian Jewry as described in the Book of Esther.

Suggested Further Reading

Amos Oz, *Israeli Literature: A Case of Reality Reflecting Fiction* (Colorado College, 1985). Insights on Israeli culture by Israel's best-known novelist.

Barry Chamish, *The Fall of Israel* (Canongate, 1992). An account of big business and Israeli corruption in the 1980s.

Benjamin Harshaw, *The Meaning of Yiddish* (University of California Press, 1992). An important history of Yiddish culture and language.

Bernard Wasserstein, *Vanishing Diaspora* (Hamish Hamilton, 1996). An examination of the recent history of the Jews of Europe focusing on the possible extinction of a Jewish presence by the mid-twenty-first century.

Blu Greenberg, *How to Run a Traditional Jewish Household* (Simon and Schuster, 1983). A readable account of Modern Orthodox Jewish practice by a well-known Jewish feminist.

David Englander, *The Jewish Enigma: An Enduring People* (Peter Halban, 1992). An overview of the community by a group of American and English scholars.

Encyclopaedia Judaica, 16 Volumes (Keter, 1971). Invaluable articles on every aspect of Judaism.

Ernst Pawel, *The Labyrinth of Exile: A Life of Theodor Herzl* (Collins Harvill, 1988). An insightful biography of the founder of modern Zionism and his times.

Geoffrey Wigoder, *The New Standard Jewish Encyclopaedia* (rev. ed., Facts On File, 1992).

Hans Küng, *Judaism* (SCM Press, 1995). An important book on early Jewish history written by the world's leading Roman Catholic liberal scholar.

Hyam Maccoby, *A Pariah People* (Constable, 1996). An interesting anthropological explanation of anti-Semitism.

Irving Howe, *The World of Our Fathers: The Journey of Eastern European Jews to America* (Schocken Books, 1990). Best-selling account of the world of Eastern European Jewry.

Isidore Fishman, *Introduction to Judaism* (Vallentine Mitchel, rev. ed. 1970). An older book, but a comprehensive introductory text of traditional Jewish belief and practice.

Jacob Neusner, *The Bavli: An Introduction* (Scholars, 1992). An indispensable guide to rabbinic Judaism written by a leading Talmudic scholar.

Jonathon Sacks, *Faith in the Future* (Longman and Todd, 1995). Reflections from the Chief Rabbi of the British Commonwealth on today's moral issues in the light of Orthodox Judaism.

Kenneth Stow, *Alienated Minority: The Jews of Medieval Latin Europe* (Harvard University Press, 1992). An interesting account of the medieval Ashkenazim community.

Leo Trepp, *The Complete Book of Jewish Observance* (Behram House, 1980). A useful, comprehensive guide to Jewish living.

Louis Jacobs, *The Jewish Religion: A Companion* (Oxford University Press, 1995). An excellent comprehensive introduction to the Jewish religion.

————, *Principles of the Jewish Faith* (rev. ed., Jason Arsonson Inc., 1988). An accessible exposition of Maimonides' principles of the Jewish faith by an eminent British scholar.

Martin Gilbert, *The Holocaust: The Jewish Tragedy* (Fontana Press, 1987). An overwhelming account of the twentieth-century Jewish tragedy. Gilbert is also the official biographer of Winston Churchill.

Michael Meyer, *Response to Modernity: History of the Reform Movement in Judaism* (Oxford University Press, 1988). A thorough history of the Reform movement.

Mitchell Bard, Ph.D., *The Complete Idiot's Guide to the Middle East Conflict* (Alpha Books, 1998). A useful text on the past and present of the Middle Eastern conflict by the Executive Director of the nonprofit organization the American-Israeli Cooperative Enterprise (AICE).

Nicholas De Lange, *Judaism* (Oxford University Press, 1987). A popular, clear, and readable introduction to Judaism.

Norman Cantor, *The Sacred Chain* (HarperCollins, 1994). A splendidly iconoclastic view of Jewish history and the Jewish future.

Norman Stillman, *The Jews of Arab Lands* (Jewish Publication Society, 1979). An excellent account of the history of Sephardic Jewry.

————, *The Jews in Arab Lands in Modern Times* (Jewish Publication Society, 1991). A fascinating history of Jews in Islamic lands since 1800.

Rabbi Benjamin Blech, *The Complete Idiot's Guide to Jewish History and Culture* (Alpha Books, 1998). Easy-to-follow coverage of all of Jewish history, including profiles of Biblical, religious, and political leaders, such as Abraham, Moses, King David, and Golda Meir.

————, *The Complete Idiot's Guide to Learning Yiddish* (Alpha Books, 2000). An excellent primer on this Eastern European language.

————, *The Complete Idiot's Guide to Understanding Judaism* (Alpha Books, 1999). Excellent introduction to all aspects of the Jewish faith.

Richard Elliot Friedman, *Who Wrote the Bible?* (Cape, 1988). A splendid summary of the findings of modern Biblical scholarship.

Richard Siegel, Michael Strassfeld, Sharon Strassfeld, *The Jewish Catalog* (Jewish Publication Society, 1973). A best-selling do-it-yourself guide to Jewish practice.

Sander Gilman, *The Jew's Body* (Routledge, 1992). A psychiatric interpretation of the role of anti-Semitism in modern culture.

Stephen Sharot, *Messianism, Mysticism, and Magic: A Sociological Analysis of Jewish Religion* (University of North Carolina Press, 1982). A discussion of mystical and messianic beliefs by an Israeli sociologist.

Susan Weidman Schneider, *Jewish and Female* (Simon & Schuster, 1984). A penetrating discussion of Judaism in the light of modern feminism.

Yael Dayan, *My Father, His Daughter* (Farrar Straus, 1985). A fascinating portrait of Israeli hero Moshe Dayan by his daughter.

Index

U–V–W

X-Y-Z